Table of Contents

Preface.

Chapter 1.   6
Re-connecting the Constitution of the
Democratic Republic of America to
Jefferson's Declaration of Independence.

Chapter 2.   26
Individual Rights and the Promotion
of the Sovereign National Economic
Interest.

Chapter 3.   50
The National Judiciary of the
Democratic Republic of America.

Chapter 4.   73
The Political Party and Election
Rules of the Democratic Republic
of America.

Chapter 5.   98
The Restoration of State Sovereignty
In the Democratic Republic of America.

Chapter 6.   131
The President's Responsibilities
in Defending National Sovereignty
and the Natural Rights of Individuals.

Chapter 7.   174
Eliminating Corporate Corruption
In the Natural Rights Republic.

Chapter 8.   194
Slavery, Racism and Secession.

Chapter 9. 231
Crossing the Rubicon to Create
the Democratic Republic of America.

Chapter 10. 242
Correcting Madison's Flawed Rules
 of Ratification.

Chapter 11. 254
The Democratic Republic of America.

Chapter 12. 270
The Constitution of the Democratic
Republic of America.

Preface

The representative republic of Madison ended in 2008, in a corrupt, oppressive centralized aristocracy of elites.

The centralized tyranny has an incipient potential for being converted to a socialist totalitarian state.

When Madison adopted part of the British constitutional class system, he truncated it to better fit the American experience of 1787.

He disconnected his constitution from the principles of natural rights in the Declaration of Independence, and omitted the British safeguards against judicial tyranny.

Without the Res Publica of natural rights, Madison's version of the British Constitution does not contain political vehicles for common citizens to alter or abolish this centralized tyranny.

Polybius described three states of government as the one, the few, and the many. Unlike Artistotle's conception of government, Polybius described a cycle, where the few would end in corruption, and be replaced by the democracy of the many.

As predicted by Polybius, Madison's representative republic ended in corruption. The subsequent government predicted by Polybius is the democracy of the many.

This book explains how to replace Madison's corrupt, aristocratic tyranny with a democratic republic.

That republic is called The Democratic Republic of America.

Chapter 1.
Re-connecting the Constitution of the Democratic Republic of America to Jefferson's Declaration of Independence.

In the natural rights individualist society, the role of government is to reduce the chance situations that other individuals, or the deep state agents, will deploy the police power of the state to override the individual citizen's freedoms of choice in pursuing their sovereign life mission.

The government serves this function by administering the rule of law provided by the constitutional framework of collective decision-making, whose goal is to secure just outcomes to the laws that individuals give to themselves.

"No one is born into moral subjugation to political power," stated Jefferson.

Jefferson wrote that when citizens leave the state of nature to create their government,

> all men are created equal… in nature all humans are equal…not subject to the rightful authority of any other human being…in a state of nature no rightful authority exists in nature. No man is subjected to the will or authority of any other man.

Jefferson believed that individuals are rights-possessors, with equal inalienable rights to pursue their own happiness, manage their private lives, and be free of government coercion in their person and their property.

Jefferson's natural rights principles were:

- Equality among citizens to participate in government.
- Privacy of citizens from the invasions of agents of government.
- The right to vote in free and fair elections.

- The protection of the natural and property rights of individuals as the supreme goal of government.
- Equal access to the courts and equality before the law.

Jefferson wrote the Declaration as a compact between citizens in each state to establish a rightful centralized political power, dedicated to protecting the natural rights of citizens that are left incompletely protected within each state government.

The adoption of the Declaration, in 1776, and the subsequent adoption of the Articles of Confederation, in 1781, moved the citizens of the United States toward a constitutional egalitarian individualism, with an appeal to natural rights.

Jefferson's constitutional arrangement, as expressed in the Articles of Confederation, was based upon the common moral values in the Declaration.

Madison's constitution was not.

Madison's constitution of 1787, replaced the first set of cultural values with his conception of the British social class system of politics.

Madison's motivation for "fixing" the Articles was based on the purported weakness in the Articles that allowed farmers to pay their taxes and their loan debt in paper money issued by the states.

Madison, and the 37 elites who signed the new constitution, wanted government debt to be paid in gold and silver, not paper money. In order to accomplish this goal, the elites had to eviscerate the legal authority of the states to issue money.

By the supreme law of the land, Madison's constitution forced the farmers to pay in gold. And, the penalty for not paying their debts in gold, was confiscation of their land by the new central government.

In re-imposing the British mixed government social class system, in 1787, Madison denied the possibility that America would ever have a common set of constitutional moral values, because he thought that the purpose of government was to balance the financial interests of one class against the other, not secure the rights of citizens from the state.

As Hamilton explained in the Federalist,

> Every community divides itself into hostile interests of the few and the many, the rich and well-born against the mass of people If either of these interests possessed all the power it would oppress the other...we (the well born) need to be rescued from the democracy.

Or, as James Dickson, one of the 37 self-selected elite "Framers" stated at the convention in 1787, the new constitution must protect "the worthy against the licentious."

Dickson explained that Madison's new Federal constitution placed the remedy in the hands (well born) which feel the disorder of democracy, whereas the antifederalists placed the remedy in the hands of citizens (the common people), who cause the disorder, by not paying their taxes and debts in gold and silver.

In other words, Madison's flawed arrangement unleashed perpetual class warfare in America, exactly as citizens see today with the rhetoric of the Democrat socialists.

Madison stacked the constitutional deck against the common class in favor of the natural aristocratic elites.

From Madison's notes,

August 12.

Mr. RANDOLPH moved, according to notice, to reconsider Article 4, Sect. 5, concerning money bills, which had been struck out. He argued, — first, that he had not wished for this privilege, whilst a proportional representation in the Senate was in contemplation: but since an equality had been fixed in that House, the large States would require this compensation at least.

Secondly, that it would make the plan more acceptable to the people, because they will consider the Senate as the more aristocratic body, and will expect that the usual guards against its influence will be provided, according to the example of Great Britain.

Thirdly, the privilege will give some advantage to the House of Representatives, if it extends to the originating only; but still more, if it restrains the Senate from amending. Fourthly he called on the smaller States to concur in the measure, as the condition by which alone the compromise had entitled them to an equality in the Senate. He signified that he should propose, instead of the original section, a clause specifying that the bills in question should be for the purpose of revenue, in order to repel the objection against the extent of the words, "raising money," which might happen incidentally; and that the Senate should not so amend or alter as to increase or diminish the sum; in order to obviate the inconveniences urged against a restriction of the Senate to a simple affirmation or negative.

Mr. WILLIAMSON seconded the motion.

Mr. PINCKNEY was sorry to oppose the opportunity gentlemen asked to have the question again opened for discussion, but as he considered it a mere waste of time he could not bring himself to consent to it. He said that, notwithstanding what had been said as to the compromise, he always considered this section as making no part of it. The rule of representation in the first branch was the true condition of that in the second branch. Several others spoke for and against the reconsideration, but without going into the merits.

Madison's precedent of meeting with a small delegation of elites in Annapolis, in 1786, to plan for his new constitution, is a valid model to follow, today.

The elites who met in Annapolis continued to serve as delegates in Philadelphia, and then served as the secret cadre of leaders who ushered in the new government.

The wealthy, natural aristocracy, at that time, also served as elected or appointed representatives in their state legislatures.

It took only 37 of them to form the new nation, and since they served a dual role in the state legislatures, they were able to shepherd the fraudulent citizen conventions through to the fraudulent ratification.

After they completed their coup, the Federalists were successful in having themselves elected to the first Congress, in order to continue their work.

Without ever mentioning rules for the operation of political parties, Madison's rules devolved into a two party straight-jacket. There are only two social classes in his scheme, and both social classes initially had their own political party.

The wealthy elites started out as Federalists, and eventually became the Republican Party. Essentially, Republicans at the national and local level relied on the Madison British class system to pursue their selfish personal interests by promoting the interests of their corporate special interests.

In translating Jefferson's moral values into the Articles, Thomas Burke, the author of the Articles, aimed at resolving six issues.

Burke proposed:

- that all sovereign power was in the states separately.

- that the federal government held "expressly" enumerated powers…that each state retains its sovereignty, freedom and independence.
- that any right which is not by this confederation "expressly" delegated to the United States in Congress assembled is retained by the states.
- Congress is to be made up of two bodies of delegates, the General Council, and Council of State, with one delegate from each state.
- All bills originate in the General Council, and are read 3 times and passed by a majority in the Council of State.
- Every law must be demonstrated to be within the powers "expressly delegated to Congress."

Thomas Paine wrote, in Common Sense,

> let us hold out the hearty hand of friendship…an open and resolute friend, and a virtuous supporter of rights of mankind and of free and independent states of America," in a non-coercive constitution, with the coercive police powers of the state.

The phrase "mutual friendship" is lifted directly from Paine, and placed, by Thomas Burke, in the Preamble of the Articles, as the basis of the new government.

Burke's intent in his Articles, was "to secure and perpetuate mutual friendship and intercourse among the people of the different States in this union."

The Articles declare the purpose of the confederation:

> the States hereby severally to enter into a firm league of friendship with each other, for their common defense, the security of their liberties, and their mutual and general welfare, binding themselves to assist each other, against all force offered to, or attacks made

upon them, or any of them, on account of religion, sovereignty, trade, or any other pretense whatever.

The Articles placed the new constitution within the context of the philosophy of the Declaration so that the words of the text could be interpreted from the historical context of a strict constructionist perspective.

The words of the Articles meant as the writers of the Articles used them, as they existed in 1776, as connected in time to the text of the Declaration.

In contrast to Burke's constitution of 1776, Madison's constitution of 1787, disconnected the constitution from the Declaration, and connected his constitution to the unwritten framework of civil government, and civil rights, in England.

When Thomas Paine commented on Madison's constitution, he said,

> it is an ill-advised attempt to replicate the British form of mixed constitution...their basis for justice becomes the balancing of particular class interests....they make it difficult for citizens to participate...it deprives citizens of private manners and public principles, and is driven by power and not consent, by coercive force and not the choices of citizens.

Natural rights patriots, in 1787, understood exactly the significance of Madison's philosophically vacuous Preamble.

The natural rights patriots, aka anti-federalists, objected to five parts of Madison's rules of procedure:

- the Necessary and Proper Clause,
- the Interstate Commerce Clause,
- the lack of term limits for Congress,
- the lack of accountability for the Federal judiciary,

- the convoluted rules for amending the constitution,

Thomas Paine explained that when Madison and Hamilton said in their Federalist Papers, that the central government needs more energy, "what they want is energy over the citizens."

"A more perfect union," said Paine, about Madison's flawed Preamble, "meant a nominal nothing without principles."

The socialists today adopt Madison's two class system and apply the Marxist rhetoric of class hatred, which is a logical outcome of Madison's vacuous Preamble.

The socialists intend to use the constitutional framework to stack the deck against common citizens, in favor of the unelected and unaccountable, deep state elites, who promote a one-world globalism.

Madison's constitution means one thing about the purpose of government to left-wing socialist judges, and an entirely different thing to conservative judges.

Both sides can claim legitimacy for their interpretation because Madison left out the purpose of his government in the Preamble.

These same set of moral, constitutional values expressed in the Declaration, are expressed in the Preamble to the new constitution, which states:

> We, the citizens of the Democratic Republic of America, establish this constitutional contract between our respective states and the National Government of the Democratic Republic of America.
>
> We solemnly swear and affirm that we establish this contract to preserve and protect the natural and civil

rights of citizens in each state, and to protect and defend the sovereignty of each state and the nation, from foreign and domestic threats.

Madison's Preamble is so vacuous that the U. S. Supreme Court has rejected the relevance of the Preamble in constitutional decisions.

In 1905, in Jacobson v. Massachusetts, the Supreme Court ruled that laws cannot be challenged or declared unconstitutional based on the Preamble.

The Court declared:

> Although that Preamble indicates the general purposes for which the people ordained and established the Constitution, it has never been regarded as the source of any substantive power conferred on the Government of the United States or on any of its Departments."

While the Federal judges do not rely on the Preamble for guidance on interpreting the text, the most significant decision by the American natural aristocracy, in history, used the fraudulent statement of "We, the people," to cement the balance of power away from the states.

In McCulloch v. Maryland (1819), the Federalist elite, Chief Justice John Marshall, stressed the importance of the government being created by "We, the people. The State of Maryland claimed that it was the state governments who formed the United States and that therefore it is the states who are sovereign.

Marshall rejected this, quoting the Preamble and declaring: "The government proceeds directly from the people; is 'ordained and established,' in the name of the people."

If the strict construction of the text had been followed, Marshall would have cited the ending paragraph.

The 37 Federalist elites, who met in secret in Philadelphia, signed their names under the text:

> Done in Convention by the Unanimous Consent of the States present the Seventeenth Day of September in the Year of our Lord one thousand seven hundred and Eighty seven and of the Independence of the United States of America the Twelfth.

It is a lie for Marshall to say that there was "unanimous consent of the states," as well as a lie for Marshall to say that the constitution proceeded directly from the people.

The constitution was signed by 37 self-selected, financially self-interested elites, who created an enduring fantasy that they were in fact, "we, the people."

There is no "people" in Madison's Preamble, or in the text of his constitution. There is only 37 elites who masqueraded as "We, the people."

Madison's Preamble states:

> We the people of the United States, in order to form a more perfect union, establish justice, insure domestic tranquility, provide for the common defense, promote the general welfare, and secure the blessings of liberty to ourselves and our posterity, do ordain and establish this Constitution for the United States of America.

Apologist academics that defend Madison's Preamble attempt to hide the flaw of "We, the people," under lofty scholarly sophistry.

For example, Michael Stokes Paulsen states that Madison's Preamble may be so intellectually sophisticated that its plain text meaning is not accessible to ordinary citizens.

Paulsen writes,

> The statement of purpose, in the Preamble, is at such a high level of generality as not to supply substantive rules of law – certainly not to supply substantive content in conflict with the substantive constitutional provisions that follow, which presumably instantiate the purposes stated in the Enactment Clause. Indeed, the statement of purposes is so general, vague, and ambiguous as not really to supply much of a rule of construction either. What is "justice"? What do the "blessings of liberty" require as a substantive matter? What is necessary to provide for the "common defense" or to assure "domestic tranquility"? What is the "general welfare?"

Paulsen suggests that the words and text are sufficient to interpret the text, in a method that Paulsen calls strict texturalism, also known as strict construction.

Without the benefit of an end goal of government in Madison's Preamble, Paulsen can not apply his method of texturalism because it yields multiple results, depending on what political party is interpreting the text.

In economic theory, Paulsen's dilemma is known as Arrow's Paradox, where the welfare benefit of an economic policy cycles over and over again, in a philosophical do-loop.

Paulsen argues that Madison's Preamble provisions

> do not "stand for" abstract principles; they "stand for" what they say. But rules or standards may not properly be deduced from the text by first illegitimately inducing it to stand for some principle that its unspecific words do not in fact justify. A text does not contain a "principle" apart from its true range of meaning. With certain texts thought to be highly general or vague, the answer might simply be that the text in fact does not supply a rule or a standard.

In other words, Paulsen argues that texturalism can proceed in the absence of the historical context of the text, in a type of ahistorical, socially-constructed reality.

In Paulsen's method of strict construction, he suggests that treating any "thing" external to the text as authoritative is not allowed. In other words, the repeated use of the term "this constitution," in Madison's text limits any interpretation of the specific written text, including the historical context of the text itself.

His method employs the objective, reasonable-person stance to reading the words of the text, without application of the context of the text. His method is a form of texturalism, without the context. A reasonable person reads the text, but must not apply logic to the historical facts of the text, at the time it was written.

The reason for this subterfuge is that the citizens had just beaten the British, (the historical context), and Madison intended to re-create the British form of government in America.

As Paulsen noted,

> strict construction is the opposite of liberal construction, which permits a term to be reasonably and fairly evaluated so as to implement the object and purpose of the document. An ongoing debate in U.S. law concerns how judges should interpret the law. Advocates of strict construction believe judges must exercise restraint by refusing to expand the law through implication. Critics of strict construction contend that this approach does not always produce a just or reasonable result.

Paulsen continues,

> constitutional supremacy implies strict textualism as a controlling method of constitutional interpretation, not free-wheeling judicial discretion. It is simply not consistent with the idea of the Constitution as binding law to adopt a hermeneutic of textualism that permits individuals to assign their own private, potentially idiosyncratic meanings to the words and phrases of the Constitution. The meaning of the words and phrases of the Constitution as law is necessarily fixed as against private assignments of meaning.

In Paulsen's method, "We, the people," is a mythical party to the contract, which established the supremacy of the British form of government. Madison's constitution is not the American form of government protecting individual freedom established in the Declaration and the first Preamble of the Articles.

For example, both the Preamble of the Articles, and the Preamble to the natural rights constitution of the Democratic Republic of America, describe the two parties to the contract as the citizens of the states and the new central, national government.

In Paulsen's strict construction method, the lawgivers who wrote the text were not really the lawgivers who wrote the text. Paulsen argues, "The lawmakers of the Constitution were "We the People," not the framers or ratifiers or anyone else."

Paulsen admits that the humans who wrote the text were not the "framers," or the "ratifiers" of the document.

He states that,

> The Constitution dictates the perspective of an abstract hypothetical collective Person, "We the People," who speak through the document itself. The text of the hypothetical "We, the

people," confirms an objective, reasonable-person stance to interpreting the words of the text. They also would seem to confirm a public stance toward constitutional interpretation. Whoever "We the People" is/are, these words plainly describe a public persona.

Paulsen argues that the objective meaning of the words, in the absence of any context, must be interpreted by some hypothetical "objective observer" or "reasonable person" who interprets the text written by some other hypothetical person, called "We, the people."

In one part of his argument, where it suits his interpretation of Madison's Preamble, Paulsen argues that Madison's Preamble provisions "do not "stand for" abstract principles; they

> stand for" what they say... A text does not contain a "principle" apart from its true range of meaning. With certain texts thought to be highly general or vague, the answer might simply be that the text in fact does not supply a rule or a standard.

In another part of his argument he switches sides and asserts that the text of Madison's constitution contains principles that allow an objective observer to apply strict construction.

Paulsen writes,

> The very purpose of a Bill of Rights was to withdraw certain subjects from the vicissitudes of political controversy, to place them beyond the reach of majorities and officials and to establish them as legal principles to be applied by the courts. One's right to life, liberty, and property, to free speech, a free press, freedom of worship and assembly, and other fundamental rights may not be submitted to vote; they depend on the outcome of no elections.

Paulsen stakes his claim for interpreting the Preamble on the use of the text, "this Constitution."

Paulsen states,

> It is "this Constitution" – a specific written text – that all officers of government swear to support and be bound by, according to its written terms. It is "this Constitution" – a specific written text – that is amended, by the addition of new written text, when amendments are adopted pursuant to the procedures specified in Article V.

The purpose of "this constitution," for Paulsen, was to usurp the authority of the Articles, and replace the Articles with text that forever embedded the financial interests of the 37 natural aristocratic elites over the financial interests of the common citizens.

Paulsen explains 3 fundamental goals of the government of 1787 that established the 240 year unfair advantage of the wealthy over the common citizens.

First, the new constitution maintained the prior public and private debts owed to the elites, but modified by "the supreme law of the land" that the new central government could compel the repayment of debts in gold and silver, not in paper money issued by the states."

Second, the new constitution stated that, "Treaties made under the Confederation are carried forward as part of the binding legal obligations of the United States under the Constitution, just as debts and contractual obligations are."

Third, the new constitution permanently eviscerated the authority of state courts in favor of establishing a superior judicial power in the central government. Paulsen makes special note of the force of this text: "Judges in every State shall be bound thereby, any Thing in the Constitution or Laws of any State to the Contrary notwithstanding."

Federal judges served for life and were approved by the natural aristocratic elites in the Senate. The Federal judges serve the interests of whatever political party that appointed them.

Paulsen concludes his argument about the purpose of Madison's constitution by noting, "This starting point yields the conclusion that discerning the lawgiver's intention is the object in reading the text. It is, in a small way, an interpretive stance external to the text, and circular in its own way."

It is circular in its own way because Madison deliberately obscured the fact that the intention of the lawgivers was to permanently establish British civil rules and procedures that benefited the elites, who wrote the text.

Just as the royalty in England derive unwarranted benefits from their unwritten constitutional text.

The circular logic of the text allows socialists to interpret the text as binding authoritative law, disconnected from the will of the citizens and not derived from the consent of the governed, to promote global socialism.

Paulsen complains that socialist judges,

> "sever the interpretive premises and principles from the text being interpreted. The more that socialist judges use their own interpretive approach the more the text is disconnected from the text's authority.

If the text's prescribed approach is textualism, following that approach connects interpretive method to the whims and vagaries of contemporary Marxist doctrine.

The deep state agents routinely deprive common citizens of due process of law, in "executive or judicial action taken without lawful authorization and/or not in accordance with traditional forms of justice."

This type of left-wing judicial interpretation deprives the elite from obtaining their just rewards, under the heavily skewed rules of the Constitution, by interpreting the text to empower the agencies of government unchecked power of the deep state elites.

Paulsen dismisses the prior authority of the Articles by noting that Madison's constitution replaced the Articles.

> The difference between constitutional interpretation and Articles-of-Confederation interpretation is that the Constitution is our governing document and the Articles of Confederation is not.

In contrast to Paulsen's ethereal method of strict construction, in the Articles, Burke wrote that,

> the authority of the congress rested on the prior acts of the several states, to which the states gave their voluntary consent, and until those obligations were fulfilled, neither nullification of the authority of congress, exercising its due powers, nor secession from the compact itself was consistent with the terms of their original pledges.

The Articles were written by Burke to be a perpetual union of the states, which is the primary reason Madison conducted his cabal to eliminate the Articles, in secret.

Madison's constitution is also intended to be perpetual.

In contrast to Madison, the new Constitution of the Democratic Republic of America embeds the set of Jefferson's principles of government directly into the text of the Preamble, so that there cannot be ambiguity about the meaning of the text.

The guiding principles of the new National Government are:

By freely and voluntarily joining our state government into the union of Democratic Republic, we affirm that the National Government will be guided by the following principles:

1. "...that all legitimate government authority is derived from the consent of the citizens governed..."

2. "...that as the consequence of the sovereign authority of citizens, citizens have an inalienable natural right to immediately remove an elected representative from office upon a referendum of 37% of registered voters in a state..."

3. "...that those governed by the laws and whose individual freedom is restricted by the laws should have the greatest say and consent in making of the laws..."

4. "...that those who make the laws and give consent to the laws, acting as representatives of the citizens, bind themselves and their constituents to following the laws..."

5. "...that the National Government is instituted to allow individual citizens to pursue individual happiness and to limit the arbitrary application of government power over the lives of individuals..."

6. "...that individual citizens who freely give their consent to form a government through constitutional conventions are bound by the original contract until the operation of the government becomes destructive to the original intent of obtaining individual freedom and the pursuit of happiness..."

7. "...that the citizens of each state have mechanisms in place in the constitutional contract to modify or abolish the governments that have been created that have become destructive to the ideals and goals under which the National Government is instituted, including the right to vote on remaining a member of the national government in a referendum to be held every 20 years from the date of admittance..."

8. "...that the parties to the constitutional contract are individual citizens acting through their elected representatives at the state and national levels of government..."

9. "...that the National Government is created by this union of states and the National Government shall never usurp the sovereign power or authority of the individual states or the sovereignty of the citizens in each state and that states have an inalienable right to call a convention of the states, without Congressional approval, to modify, amend, or abolish this Constitutional Contract."

10. "...that an individual's private property obtained through legal contract and title transfer, their rights to appropriate income and profits from the use of their private property, and their rights to dispose and transfer their private property are inviolate and derived from natural rights granted to them by God, and that no government or constitutional contract may ever abrogate or subordinate these natural individual rights, unless by free and voluntary consent of the citizen..."

11. "...that a citizens Grand Jury of 18 citizens is impaneled, for a term of 12 months, to protect and preserve the rights of citizens against the arbitrary application of government power against citizens..."

12. "...that a citizens Grand Jury of 18 citizens must inspect all national penal facilities within its

district every 6 months, and report their findings to the Chief District Judge, who shall act to remedy the deficiencies found by the Grand Jury…"

13. "…that the 1776 American experiment of representative democracy was ordained by God to pursue individual human freedoms and liberty from oppression and is an exceptional model in human history to be preserved, protected, and cherished by the citizens and deployed by them and their elected representatives as the guiding principles in the Democratic Republic of America in its relationships with other nations and other people…"

The text of the new constitution follows the framework and text of many of the state governments, that Madison's constitution eviscerated with his centralized government that had power over states.

The set of principles in the new constitution is the single arrangement of constitutional authority that leads the nation to the highest rates of economic growth and prosperity because it allows citizens maximum freedom to "pursue their own happiness," an outcome that Madison and Hamilton intended to avoid at all costs.

Chapter 2.
Individual Rights and the Promotion of the Sovereign National Economic Interest.

Beginning around 1796, Madison's Constitution generated periodic, recurring national economic crises, at an interval of about every 10 years.

The instability in the U. S. economy is precipitated by speculation in assets, inflation, monetary instability, and tax and fiscal policies that adversely affect national aggregate demand.

The financial elites in America are the economic agents who precipitate the economic instability with their asset speculation, and the concomitant power to affect monetary policy, to their own benefit.

Because Madison's Constitution stacked the deck against common citizens, they have suffered needless financial distress during the economic crises. Madison's system of checks and balances left common citizens defenseless to represent their own social class interests in the economic downturns.

In contrast, the natural aristocracy have sailed through most recessions largely unscathed because Madison's rules tended to insulate the elite from the consequences of their wild speculative schemes and unbalanced monetary policy.

Because of their unbalanced constitutional power, they have been able to use the agencies and resources of government to avoid financial distress.

As in the 2008 case of the U. S. Government bailouts of banks and global corporations, throughout the history of the nation, Madison's rules allowed the elites to manipulate government tax and financial policy to benefit the elite financial interests.

Eventually, the flaws in Madison's rules allowed the corporate and financial elite to disconnect their government welfare benefits from the consent of the governed.

The correct description of this political arrangement is called "centralized elite tyranny." It is also called "the deep state."

In his excellent article titled, "America's Ruling Class — And the Perils of Revolution," Angelo M. Codevilla explains how the elites in the swamp operate their tyranny, outside the rule of law.

Codevilla used the example of how the elites used tax money to bail themselves out of the global financial crisis, in the Fall of 2008.

Codevilla wrote,

> the leaders of the Republican and Democratic parties, agreed that spending $700 billion to buy the investors' "toxic assets" was the only alternative to the U.S. economy's "systemic collapse." In this, President George W. Bush and his would-be Republican successor John McCain agreed with the Democratic candidate, Barack Obama.

The decisions by the elites, in 2008, were reached in secret. The decisions primarily benefited three large investment banks, who are the main movers and shakers of the unelected, unaccountable, deep state agents in the swamp.

The reason that the deep state elites in the swamp operate their cabal in secret is to direct the world's economic and financial benefits to themselves.

Codevilla's analysis explains that within Madison's two political party British social class system, the Vichy Republicans collaborate with Obama's socialist Democrat Party to serve the corporate elite interests.

As he notes, "No prominent Republican challenged the ruling class's continued claim of superior insight, nor its denigration of the American people as irritable children who must learn their place. The Republican Party did not disparage the ruling class, because most of its officials are or would like to be part of it."

In other words, there are not two political parties that represent distinct social classes, as intended by Madison's British mixed government model.

Both political parties, for different reasons, promote globalization of the American economy, to the detriment of the sovereign national economic interest.

The elites in the swamp, under Madison's flawed constitution, did not need to capture political control in all 250 metro regions, they just needed to get unchecked political control of both political parties in Washington, in order to collude and rig the global economic system for their own interests.

Globalization of the American economy, in other words, should be seen in the bigger context of the rule of law and the evisceration of the sovereignty of America, as a distinct nation.

The three large global investment banks have a strangle-hold on the rate of capital investment in the U. S. domestic economy that allows the bankers to manage the global economy in order to reward themselves.

They choose when, how, and where capital investment will occur in the global economy.

Totalitarian political control of the rate of capital investment, in the hands of the global investment banks, reduces the need for the elites to seek any form of the consent of the governed to exert total control over the economy.

Under a different set of constitutional rules, a different set of national economic outcomes would be obtained.

There is no justification for Madison's rules that inflict damage on common citizens by precipitating perpetual cyclical economic crisis.

The economic instability in the American economy is not a "naturally-occurring" adjustment to economic equilibrium. It is a Madison-made unfair and unbalanced system of rules that benefits the "natural aristocracy."

Madison's rules could be replaced with constitutional rules that did not generate economic instability.

James Buchanan, the late professor of economics at James Mason University, explained how the constitutional rules affected the nation's rate of economic growth.

Under one set of constitutional rules, Buchanan predicted certain types of economic outcomes. Under a different configuration of rules, Buchanan predicted another type of economic outcome.

Buchanan argued that there is only one, unique, configuration of constitutional rules that leads the nation to optimum rates of national economic growth. These rules aim at maximum individual freedom to allow individuals to seek their own happiness.

Following the work of Buchanan, this chapter compares and contrasts the economic outcomes under 3 sets of constitutional rules:

The Articles of Confederation, first created in 1776, and adopted, by 13 states in 1781, as the nation's first constitution.

The natural rights constitution of the Democratic Republic of America, first proposed in 2018.

The three constitutional arrangements can be compared based upon how each constitution resolves 4 national economic growth issues that generate conflicts of financial interests among political and social classes.

One set of interests promotes the national sovereign economic interest.

The other side promotes corporate globalism, which directs economic benefits to global banks and corporations.

About 15% of the U. S. domestic economy benefits from the global elite tyranny.

There are three major primary investment banks that direct the global activity and only about 1500 large corporations that are connected to the global financial transactions.

The other 85% of the population are powerless to change this status quo because Madison's rules provide no mechanism for the citizens to regain the consent of the governed.

Summary of the Four Conflicts of Interest Between Constitutional Rules.

Flows of technical information within national sovereign borders.	Open flows to create wide range of new ventures.	Private, proprietary flows to absorb internal benefits of technology innovation
Flows of new technology ventures creation.	Open flows, maximum new venture creation.	Limited flows in order to protect global corporate core competency.
Pathway of technical change.	Maximum technical change and greatest diversity in new venture creation.	Technical change directed to global corporation's core competency.
Cultural/political values.	Individual freedom, reward based upon individual merit, maximum individual risk-taking.	Globalist/collectivist values oriented to using government to promote resolution of market-based conflicts.

Buchanan explained that every set of constitutional rules has an internal end-goal to which the rules are directed.

In Logical Foundations of Constitutional Liberty, (1999), Buchanan relies on a philosophy of logic to explain how the end goals of a constitution, clearly stated in the preamble, create the binding allegiance of citizens to follow the rule of law.

One set of interests promotes the national sovereign economic interest.

The other side promotes corporate globalism, which directs economic benefits to global banks and corporations.

About 15% of the U. S. domestic economy benefits from the global elite tyranny.

There are three major primary investment banks that direct the global activity and only about 1500 large corporations that are connected to the global financial transactions.

The other 85% of the population are powerless to change this status quo because Madison's rules provide no mechanism for the citizens to regain the consent of the governed.

Buchanan reasoned that constitutional rules were required to reduce the chance situation that a citizen would be subjected to the arbitrary police power of the state.

He wrote, "Uncertainty about just where one's own interest will lie in a sequence of plays or rounds will lead a rational person, from his own interest, to prefer rules and arrangements, or constitutions that will seem fair, no matter what final positions he might occupy."

His first principle of logic is that all individuals are rational in the pursuit of their own sovereign life mission,

In The Theory of Public Choice, (1972), he defines an individual not so much from the perspective of insight-imagination, but from the brain's rational choice attribute.

He states that,

> ...we can simply define a person in terms of his set of preferences, his utility function. This function defines or describes a set of possible trade-offs among alternatives for potential choice.

In The Reason of Rules. (2000), Buchanan explains the importance of how citizens provide prior consent to follow the rules that they give to themselves.

"Just conduct," writes Buchanan, "consists of behavior that does not violate rules to which one has given prior consent."

In other words, rather than relying on the separation of powers to deal with the problem of special interests, as Madison did, Buchanan relies upon the rationality of self-interest as a force that binds individuals to society as a process of rationally minimizing risk in uncertain decision making environments.

In leaving the state of nature, and forming a constitution, Buchanan explains, individuals are placed in a position of uncertainty in the outcome of their life's mission. No individual knows in advance where the individual may end up, given the choice between one set of constitutional rules or another.

His logic of individual rationality is that any individual, with a rational self-interest, would choose fair rules for all, aimed at the greatest freedom for all.

In constitutional decision-making under uncertainty, individuals would seek rules that had maximum equal rights for all, with special privileges for none. The end goal, or telos, of the constitution, in this case of rational self-interest, is individual freedom.

Buchanan wrote,

> To the extent that Madison's constitution commands little respect, it is, in part, because it fails in its function of limiting the scope of both governmental and private intrusion into what are widely held to be protected spheres of activity.

Madison's constitution was not based upon the prior consent of the citizens, while the Articles of Confederation obtained the prior consent of the 13 states, who promised to be bound by the perpetual rules.

Madison's flaw of not obtaining the prior consent of the citizens was compounded by his deliberately vague statement of the end goals in the Preamble. "To form a more perfect union" could mean anything, as Thomas Paine and George Mason, pointed out, at the time.

There was no "We, the people," at the creation of Madison's constitution. There were only 37 self-selected political and financial elites, who met in secret to draft the rules.

"We, the people is actually just 37 elites who had the audacity to call themselves, "We, the people."

While Madison promised that the central government would not operate directly on citizens in each state, his constitution allowed the central government to operate directly upon the citizens, without providing the mechanism for citizens to enforce the rule of law on the law-givers.

The operation of the central government directly on the citizens violated Buchanan's first principle of justice.

In The Reason of Rules, Buchanan and Brennan write,

> Our specific claim is that justice takes its meaning from the rules for the social order within which

> notions of justice are to be applied. To appeal to considerations of justice is to appeal to relevant rules. These rules provide the framework within which patterns of distributional end states emerge from the interaction of persons who play various complex functional roles.

In other words, fair distribution of income and wealth, under Buchanan, is obtained through just rules of financial and economic exchange.

Buchanan's interpretation of justice as fair rules is dramatically different than Madison's rules of civil procedure. Madison's notion of justice relies on a set of judicial elites who judge the fairness of welfare outcomes, after a transaction has occurred, and a dispute arises between the parties.

Once confirmed by the Senate, the Federal judicial elites cannot be removed by the citizens because the judges are appointed for life. Their decisions about just outcomes, throughout U. S. economic history, have been slanted to the benefit of the elites.

Buchanan applies his concept of justice to his suggestions about the relationship between free markets and governmental power. He states that

> ...for most persons, the independence offered by the presence of market alternatives offers the maximal liberty possible. But we have not yet designed institutions that will satisfy the individual's search for community in the impersonal setting of the market order without, at the same time, undermining the very independence that this order afford.

The point he is making is that a certain type of institutional arrangement in government rules damages individual freedom gained in the free market. This lesson has been learned over and over again, by the common citizens, as in the case of farmers during the debt-peonage era.

The farmers were making a moral argument about justice and fairness. The Federal judges were answering the argument from the perspective of economic rules of civil procedure. Madison's constitution does not contain principles of justice and fairness.

It only contains rules of civil procedure. In the application of those rules, taking away the land of the farmers was a civil right of the bankers.

Buchanan addressed this question of fairness in his book The Theory of Public Choice, when he described the difference between "economic man," and "moral man."

Economic man, according to Buchanan, is defined by his utility function, whose variables are weighted according to their contribution to monetary wealth.

"Economic man's behavior," notes Buchanan, "in the economic relationship is not influenced by ethical or moral considerations that serve to constrain his pursuit of his objectively defined interest."

Under a different constitutional arrangement, economic man's pursuit of unfair advantage would be tempered by the presence of moral man's principles of justice in the distribution of welfare benefits.

As Buchanan notes, the welfare outcomes that the elites seek to maximize are their own, not the welfare outcomes that benefit the national sovereign economic interests. Once the elites in the swamp obtained unchecked power, they were free to escape from the burdens of the democratic consent of the governed.

Madison's flaw creates a defect in American model of democratic representative government.

Buchanan and Brennan wrote extensively on the theory of democracy as it relates to the development of fair economic laws and financial rules.

They emphasized that the development of fair rules is a political process, that is mediated by democratic procedures, in which the citizens express the consent of the governed.

In other words, after the citizens gave their prior consent to the initial creation of the rules, fair rules would allow them to give ongoing consent, after the government had been established.

Appeals to justice take place within the political system of democratic representative government, and Jefferson wrote that citizens have a God-given right to alter or abolish those rules when their application becomes destructive of the ends for which it was created.

Madison's flaw was to leave out of his constitution the end goals for which the government was created. His constitution established civil rules of procedure, without end goals.

The subsumed unstated end goals turned out to be rules that benefited the 37 elites, who met in secret, and called themselves "We, the people."

Madison's constitution ended up in a centralized elite tyranny that benefited the globalist corporate elite interests and did not promote of the sovereign national economic interest.

As Buchanan has pointed out, a different configuration of constitutional rules would produce different economic outcomes.

The single, unique configuration of rules that produce maximum economic outcomes, according to Buchanan, were fair rules of exchange, based upon maximum individual freedom.

The relationship between constitutional individual freedom and national economic growth is through the ability of individuals to create new technology ventures that commercialize new technology products.

The new technology products create new future markets that create new flows of income.

Technical change causes new income flows to be created where none had existed before. Part of the new income is a result of increased productivity, meaning that output increases with reduced inputs in the production unit.

Part of the new income is in the form of profits related to new goods produced by new production units.

Another part of the income is in the form of wages and salaries paid to people who work in the new units, who spend their incomes in the local economy, creating income and employment multipliers.

There is nothing preordained or certain in the outcome of technical change that it would automatically create more future wealth or greater income.

Schumpeter explained that there are social, political, and economic forces that favor one type of technical change, and there are other political forces that favor status quo technical change.

National economic growth is a contingent outcome of the type of technical change, in the economy. It occurs in some nations, but not in others.

In The Lever of Riches: Technological Creativity and Economic Progress, (1990), Joel Mokyr reviews the relationship between economic development and technological innovation by first raising the question why economic growth occurs in some societies and not in others.

According to Mokyr, economic growth results from open flows of innovation, which only occur under one configuration of constitutional rules advocated by Buchanan.

According to Mokyr, technological progress tends to occur in national economies which have well-educated citizens, who are deeply engaged in the economic and political decisions of their communities.

In such a society, the appearance of technical progress is rapidly diffused, and as the knowledge embodied in the change spreads among citizens, it creates imbalances and bottlenecks in existing interindustry relations.

These imbalances are important as an explanation of technical change because they create the conditions for new interindustry relationships as the imbalances and bottlenecks are overcome.

The new interindustry relationships tend to create new sources of income that are not dependent on the older interindustry relationships.

Mokyr found in his historical review that certain political organizations and social groups are opposed to open knowledge flows because that type of technical change would tend to disrupt the advantages they receive from the existing status quo arrangement of power.

The status quo of power is what Madison's constitutional rules are designed to protect. In other words, Madison's constitution protects the same set of elite corporate classes in America today, as it protected the natural aristocracy, in 1787.

The accumulation of technological knowledge and the pace of technical change, are contingent outcomes of the social and political institutional structure of a region.

For technological progress to occur, according to Mokyr, "…it must be born into a socially sympathetic environment."

The strangle-hold of the investment banks on the rate of capital investment is a tool of control over the pace of technical change.

The Articles of Confederation and the natural rights constitution of the Democratic Republic of America create this type of individualistic, open flow of knowledge that is sympathetic to technical change.

Nothing about this economic relationship between technical change and economic growth has changed since 1957, when Robert Solow published his research, "Technical Change and the Aggregate Production Function."

While conventional macro economic theory of productivity improvements can explain around 25% of national economic growth, Solow showed that technical change explained about 75% of American economic growth, over 4 decades.

Joseph Schumpeter had explained, 20 years before Solow, that individualistic entrepreneurial technical change produced certain types of economic outcomes, while corporate monopolistic technical change produced a different outcome.

These two types of technical change roughly parallel the two types of constitutions under consideration in this article. Madison's constitution ended up promoting global corporate technical change.

Buchanan's constitutional rules, as applied in the Articles of Confederation and the natural rights constitution of the Democratic Republic of America promote individualistic, entrepreneurial technical change.

The two types of technical change are the major variables in understanding the resolution of the 4 conflicts of interest in the diagram, above in Part 1.

The type of technical change influences the path of national economic development. The two types of technical change tend to diffuse knowledge along different business-social networks.

One type of technical exchange produces open flows of knowledge. The other type of technical change diffuses technical knowledge in closed, proprietary flows of knowledge.

The diagram describes the different flows of knowledge.

Flows of technical information within national sovereign borders.	Open flows to create wide range of new ventures.	Private, proprietary flows to absorb internal benefits of technology innovation

The entire process of economic growth caused by open flows of knowledge can be seen as the shifting of the national production function outward, which is reflected by changing technical coefficients in a dynamic input-output model the national economy.

Economic growth caused by technical change is a result of capital investments made by entrepreneurs in new production units create new interindustry relationships and new market relationships that did not exist before.

The new ventures produce products whose supply varies, according to the feedback mechanism of consumer preferences.

The consumer demand is evolving over time and could not have been predicted by the entrepreneur because part of the new demand is based upon relationships in complementary markets, that did not exist, and are being created as a result of technical change.

One predominate conflict of interest between the globalist model and the individualist model concerns a stable monetary system.

Technical change in the individualist model requires individual risk-taking, rewards based upon individual merit, and individual creativity.

A stable national monetary policy provides a context of financial stability for the entrepreneur as he makes his guesses about the future demand for his products. If the supply of money is stable or rising, the economic conditions are favorable for continued technical change.

As long as the entrepreneur can see the conditions of stability, he has the confidence to make his guess and move forward with his capital investment into a very uncertain future.

Money supply is linked to technical change through its effect on entrepreneur's expectations on the future.

If the entrepreneur does not see stable economic conditions sufficient to make his new investment, then the rate of capital investment will cause economic decline in the future because future intermediate markets of relationships and complementary ventures are not created, that result from capital investment.

Capital investments today by entrepreneurs affect the rate of profits and the rate of economic growth in the future.

National monetary policy can create the conditions for either national economic stagnation and decline or future economic growth.

The speculative investments in assets by the elites creates unstable economic conditions. For elites, the manipulation of the money supply and interest rates is seen as a tool to use to bail themselves out of the economic crisis that they create.

In the closed, corporate global model of technical change, the production coefficients do not change, for long periods of time, because the income and employment multipliers are absorbed internally within the global corporate business networks.

In the closed, corporate model, as the eight years of Obama show, or the past 40 years of the EU, economic growth stagnates at a very low levels of economic activity.

In his early writings, Joseph Schumpeter described the internal dynamic forces of the free market as akin to the "gales of creative destruction."

There is nothing about the "gales of creative destruction" that is appealing to global financial interests who benefit from a stable technical change status quo.

In his later work, he became pessimistic about the trends that he saw in the free market which he thought were leading to oligopoly and monopoly. He was concerned that the dominant powerful firms would limit technological innovations in order to reap greater profits from their status quo position.

The business-social network that Schumpeter identified with monopoly was comprised of old production units, commercial bankers, institutional money, and senior management of branch plants of multi-national corporations.

Schumpeter explained that this corporate network had financial interests in maintaining the status quo because uncertainty upset the flow of benefits that they achieve from the status quo arrangement of power.

In Schumpeter's economic model of 1935, commercial bankers

> ...supplied the entrepreneurs with purchasing power by furnishing them with credit. Moreover, because bankers are not able to create credit in unlimited

> quantities, they have to select from among the investment plans put forward by entrepreneurs that they regard as desirable or likely to succeed.

Schumpeter continued,

> The direction that the economy will follow will depend on the investment plans that are chosen, and therefore, it is bankers who constitute the selection committees for investment plans; they are the helmsmen of the capitalist economy.

Schumpeter feared that significant technological innovations would only occur in large multi-national corporations that had sufficient resources to conduct extensive research and development.

Schumpeter thought that the multi-national corporations would be motivated to use technical change to enhance their monopoly position in the world market.

Schumpeter offered the most compelling explanation of the current global corporatist political deep state political strategy.

In the current global economy, directed by 3 large investment banks, global corporations use the pace of technical change to enhance their monopoly power.

Charles Kindleberger, in World Economic Primacy, (1996), noted how a certain set of cultural values tended to favor an attitude towards technical innovation. He characterized this attitude as the

> ...capability and will of individuals, companies and governments to break free of existing habits, perceptions, institutions, and task allocations, in order to revise them in light of constantly changing circumstances and developments.

Like Mokyr, Buchanan and Schumpeter, Kindleberger perceived a type of contingent relationship between the cultural values that support individual freedom and national economic growth.

He found that individuals in some societies have the freedom to break free of existing habits, perceptions, and institutions in order to revise their behavior in light of changing economic conditions.

In other societies, Kindleberger found a type of economic control exercised over individuals that inhibited changed behavior. Some political organizations with a vested financial interest in maintaining the status quo arrangement of power tended to oppose technical change, and thus acted to limit individual economic freedom.

The diagram describes the different cultural values.

Cultural/political values.	Individual freedom, reward based upon individual merit, maximum individual risk-taking	Globalist/collectivist values oriented to using government to promote resolution of market-based conflicts.

With the increasing trends toward an internationalization of trade and a convergence towards macro-technologies in multi-national production units, the explanation offered by the four economists suggest that agents of the deep state will maintain control over the pace of technical change as a tool to control economic growth that benefits their own corporate interests.

The elected leaders and agents in the deep stated do not have a fiduciary allegiance toward the promotion of self-sustaining national economic growth.

Madison's constitution did not require that of the elites.

His constitution failed to state, in the Preamble, whose interests the deep state agents were supposed to represent.

His rules were designed to establish rules of civil procedure to adjudicate conflicts between the two social classes, not promote maximum individual freedom and economic growth.

The public purpose in an individualist society is served by promotion and adherence to common external values of trust, fair dealing, truthful representations, and promise keeping.

Voluntary cooperation between individuals occurs when the individuals assume, prior to entering into any political or financial exchange process, that other citizens share these common cultural and political values.

As Buchanan points out, voluntary allegiance to the rule of law results from the realization that it is in one's best interest for his or her life's mission to be consistent with the public purpose of the rule of law.

The entire edifice of voluntary compliance to the rule of law is built on the principles stated in the Preamble of the Natural Rights Constitution of the Democratic Republic of America.

The Preamble states:

> We, the citizens of the Democratic Republic of America, establish this constitutional contract between our respective states and the National Government of the Democratic Republic of America.
>
> We solemnly swear and affirm that we establish this contract to preserve and protect the natural and civil rights of citizens in each state, and to protect and defend the sovereignty of each state and the nation, from foreign and domestic threats.

It is from this Preamble that the Constitutional rules that follow promote individual freedom and the national economic sovereignty.

The economic rules create the conditions for resolving the four conflicts of interest between a natural rights constitution and Madison's British mixed government constitution that aims at amelioration of conflicts between two social classes.

- Open flows of technological information to create a wide range of new ventures.
- Open flows of venture capital to create maximum rates of new venture creation.
- Maximum rate of technical change to create maximum knowledge diffusion.
- Maximum individual freedom, reward based upon individual merit to create a "sympathetic environment" for risk-taking.

The natural rights constitution has 11 provisions which establish the framework of economic freedom:

The National Congress shall have the power to issue government bonds, and to borrow money on the credit of the Democratic Republic of America. All proposals to borrow money or issue debt shall occur once in the two year budget cycle, and all proposals to issue debt must be approved by 50% of the State legislatures of the Democratic Republic of America, no later than January 21 of the year of issuance.

The term of debt and interest on any issuance of debt shall not exceed 10 years, and must be paid in full by the end of the 10th year.

The National Congress shall have the power to regulate commerce and approve trade agreements with foreign nations, which are negotiated by the President.

The National Congress shall have the power to establish a uniform rule of citizen naturalization, and provide revenues for national border security to prohibit illegal entrance into the sovereign nation or any sovereign state.

The National Congress shall have the power to coin money, regulate the value thereof, regulate the circulation and creation of money and money instruments, regulate the national banking system and establish the currency value of foreign coin, and fix the Standard of Weights and Measures.

The National Congress shall have the power to provide for the punishment for the national criminal felony of counterfeiting the securities and money of the Democratic Republic of America.

The National Congress shall have the power to establish a national Post Office and a national system of roads and transportation routes.

The National Congress shall have the power to authorize regional capital securities markets, and to establish regulatory guidelines for the operation of regional private and public security exchanges designed to promote maximum national and regional economic growth rates.

The National Congress shall have the power to establish and maintain a national patent office to promote the progress of science and useful arts, by securing for limited times to authors and inventors the exclusive right to their respective writings and discoveries.

The National Congress shall have the power to protect the patents of citizens from foreign and domestic criminal usurpation of the right of citizens to enjoy the benefits of their invention.

The National Congress shall have the power to define and punish intellectual property piracies and criminal patent felonies committed against citizens of the

Democratic Republic of America by foreign and domestic criminals.

Three of the rules are aimed at protecting intellectual property rights of inventors and entrepreneurs, so that they can reap their rewards from their individual creativity and initiative.

One of the provisions aims at creating a new capital market infrastructure in each major metro region that raises and directs capital investment into the new ventures within that region.

Three of the provisions aim at the creation and management of a stable national monetary system that limits the ability of the agents of government from unstable monetary policy.

A stable national monetary policy provides the institutional context of financial stability for the entrepreneur as he makes his guesses about the future demand for his products.

Money supply is linked to technical change through its effect on the entrepreneur's expectations on the future.

As long as the entrepreneur can see the conditions of monetary stability, he has the confidence to make his guess and move forward with his capital investment into a very uncertain future.

The Natural Rights Constitution of the Democratic Republic of America promotes a relationship between the cultural values that support individual freedom and technological change that causes national economic growth.

The shared cultural values are commonly-held external values of trust, fair dealing, truthful representations, and promise keeping.

Citizens in America today do not share this set of common cultural values. Madison's constitution devolved into an unelected, unaccountable elite tyranny that advocates globalism, not the sovereign national economic interest.

In other words, there are not two political parties that represent distinct social classes, as intended by Madison's British mixed government model.

Both political parties, for different reasons, promote globalization of the American economy, to the detriment of the sovereign national economic interest.

National economic growth is caused by capital investments in technical change made by entrepreneurs in new production units that create new interindustry relationships and new market relationships that did not exist before.

Voluntary allegiance to the rule of law, in the natural rights republic results from the fact that all citizens have an equal opportunity for upward mobility and individual prosperity by creating their own entrepreneurial ventures.

The Natural Rights Constitution promotes allegiance to the rule of law by protecting an individual's God-given natural right to pursue their own happiness.

Chapter 3.
The National Judiciary of the Democratic Republic of America.

In his transformation of the American constitution from a natural rights republic, based on Jefferson's Declaration, to the British social class mixed government, Madison had to modify the locus of "sovereignty" from individual citizens to the natural aristocracy of America.

The British "rule of law" is based upon unwritten documents that provide judges with guidance on decisions about sovereignty, based upon English common law tradition.

The British monarchy, and their associated upper crust of British society, obtain a position of privilege in the law from the unwritten common law, beginning with the Magna Carta, created as an exclusive right for the British nobility.

Madison's vacuous maximand, "more perfect union" provided the 37 elites, who signed Madison's unfair rules, a perfectly malleable document for the ensuing generations of Federalist elite judges to skew their decisions about sovereignty to the benefit of America's upper crust.

Madison's Constitution, relocated national "sovereignty" by making two changes in the Articles of Confederation.

First, Madison changed the parties to the contract from a confederation of 13 states to a central national government, whose Federal judges had ultimate sovereignty over state courts.

Second. Madison changed the terms of elected representation from a congress of state delegates, who represented the citizens of their respective states, to a centralized congress of representatives who represented their social class financial interests.

Madison's Constitution creates a government whose judiciary is the ultimate judge of whose sovereign interests are served by the constitutional rules of procedure.

Madison promised that the Federal government would not operate directly upon citizens, and that his branches of the government, legislative, executive and judicial, would check and balance each other.

Madison's flaw is that the Supreme Court, as a result of Marbury, is the ultimate power of the federal government over the other branches of government.

The judicial decisions operate directly upon citizens.

In a dispute between the federal government and the natural rights of citizens, the Federal judges base their decisions on protecting the sovereignty of the natural aristocracy.

Unlike the citizens in England, the U. S. citizens have no way of removing the tyrannical Federal judges.

For decades, after the decision in Marbury, the Federal judges based their rulings about sovereignty on their traditional interpretation of social class interests. Either side could possibly win at the Supreme Court, depending on whether there was a majority of Democrats or Republicans.

Madison's malleable document cannot be interpreted in so-called "strict construction," because the text hides the fact that the locus of sovereignty resides in the social class interests of America's natural aristocracy.

John C. Calhoun pointed out,

> strict construction is a 'phantom, a thing 'good in the abstract, but in practice not worth a farthing. Everybody is for strict construction but in fact, it will ever be found to be the construction of the permanent

minority against the permanent majority, and of course of itself valueless.

Madison's concept of tyranny was that the common citizens would obtain majority power, and exploit the tiny minority of wealthy Americans.

In the hands of Federalist Republican judges, the Court sanctions the priority of financial and property rights of America's natural aristocracy, representing the elite corporate interests of the Republican Party.

The decisions by the progeny of the Federalists led to decisions like Dred Scott.

In Dred Scott, Madison's vacuous document allowed the Federalist judges to manufacture a right of slave-owners to hold property in slaves. A strict construction of the text would not find language about the property rights of the Plantation elites to own slaves, or the legal obligation of states to capture runaway slaves, and return them to their rightful owners.

Taney's decision was based upon Madison's concept of tyranny.

The Supreme Court was protecting the property rights of minority slaveholders against the tyranny of a moralistic majority who would deprive the Plantation elite of their property rights.

In the 1896 case of Plessy v. Ferguson, the progeny of the Federalist judges on the Supreme Court manufactured legally sanctioned racial segregation.

Plessy was the case that established "separate but equal" as the Supreme law of the land. The constitutional goal of racial apartheid was to embody and reinforce an ideology of white supremacy.

But, not just any whites.

The goal of white supremacy was to establish the unchecked power of elites, over both blacks and common whites.

The text of Madison's document buries the justification of this outcome in his convoluted rules of procedural justice.

But, racial apartheid is a logical and defensible legal decision flowing from Madison's rules that relocated sovereignty in the hands of the natural aristocracy.

As Jefferson wrote,

> It is a very dangerous doctrine to consider the judges as the ultimate arbiters of all constitutional questions. It is one which would place us under the despotism of an oligarchy.

In the majority hands of progressive Democrats, the Supreme Court has manufactured rights on behalf of the common citizens.

In Griswold v. Connecticut, (1965), Justice William O. Douglas wrote for the Democrat majority that the right to abortion was to be found in the "penumbras" and "emanations" of other constitutional protections, such as the self-incrimination clause of the Fifth Amendment.

Douglas wrote, "Would we allow the police to search the sacred precincts of marital bedrooms for telltale signs of the use of contraceptives?"

By a vote of 7–2, the Democrat majority of the Supreme Court invalidated Connecticut's abortion law on the grounds that it violated the "right to marital privacy." The ruling established the constitutional basis for the right to privacy with respect to intimate practices.

This decision about protecting sexual behavior, based upon the right to privacy from governmental intrusion, formed the basis of other decisions regarding gay marriage and the rights of gay people to impose on others, the obligation to bake a wedding cake.

One of the decisions flowing from Griswold was Justice Harry Blackmun's decision, 8 years later, in Roe.

In Roe, the U. S. Supreme Court overrode the sovereignty of the Texas Court, to forbid abortion.

In a subsequent majority decision on abortion, Blackmun expressed his personal opinion.

> Few decisions are more personal and intimate, more properly private, or more basic to individual dignity and autonomy, than a woman's decision – with the guidance of her physician and within the limits specified in Roe – whether to end her pregnancy. A woman's right to make that choice freely is fundamental.

From a liberal's personal opinion, Blackmun's decision in Roe is perfectly logical and defensible. But, it is not based in the text of Madison's constitution.

The fact that the Court can fluctuate between protecting the rights of the elite when Republicans hold the majority, or protecting the rights of common citizens when Democrats are the majority, means that there is no possibility of strict construction of the text.

The document means whatever the judges want it to mean. Either side is correct. The goal of the rulings is to subordinate state courts.

Up until 2008, when Obama converted the Democrats into a global socialist party, the decisions of the Federal judges were based upon the British two-class, two party political system.

Republican judges protected the property rights of the natural aristocracy, now in the form of the corporate elite.

Democrat judges protected the rights of common working class citizens.

After Obama, the entire justification for Madison's two class system of checks and balances was rendered meaningless.

Rather than protecting the rights of common citizens, the Democrat Federal judges, at every level, based their decisions on the sovereignty of global socialism.

In other words, in changing the constitutional logic for the existence of the Democrat party, Obama relocated sovereignty from Madison's natural aristocracy to a global government sovereignty.

Because of Madison's flaw, the national sovereignty has been replaced by the ideology of globalist socialism.

The shift in national sovereignty that results from Obama's conversion of the Democrat Party to a global socialist party is enabled by the class-based ideology of the Federalist elites who wrote the constitution.

Their ideology empowered the natural aristocracy to use the judicial system as a weapon to gain their unfair advantages in a legal system that was superior to all other branches of government.

Their ideology is a type of totalitarianism that is based upon their notion that the natural aristocracy possessed "virtue." The moral quality of virtue empowered the elites to eliminate political positions that were contrary to their elite legal privileges.

The only additional step the socialists need to gain control of the judicial machinery is to substitute the moral quality of natural aristocracy "virtue" with their own ideology of their superior moral quality of "social justice."

The machinery of the centralized judicial elite tyranny would function under either ideology.

In just 12 years after the fraudulent ratification of the Constitution, the Federalist attempted to eliminate political opposition with the enactment of the Alien and Sedition Acts.

Sedition, in this case, meant political statements that were critical of the federalist elites.

The privileges of the natural aristocracy were not secure at that point in history, which was the impetus of Marshall to embed judicial supremacy as the ultimate supreme law of the land, in his 1803 decision on Marbury.

When Madison implemented the British judicial system, he failed, deliberately, to implement the British check against a judicial tyranny.

But, from the perspective of Marshall, the absence of a check was not adequate to permanently secure the elite privileges.

As noted by Brutus, a natural rights proponent during the ratification debates,

> The framers of this constitution appear to have followed that of the British, in rendering the judges independent, by granting them their offices during good behaviour, without following the constitution of England, in instituting a tribunal in which their errors may be corrected; and without adverting to this, that the judicial under this system have a power which is above the legislative, and which indeed transcends any power before given to a judicial by any free government under heaven.

The Federalist ideology created the government machinery for a centralized judicial tyranny, without ever stating the ideological goal of the machinery.

That machinery was as effective in the hands of the natural aristocracy, as it would be for the Democrats, and eventually for global socialists, who desired to create a "more perfect socialist state."

The machinery for tyranny was created in a series of actions taken by the Federalists that culminated in Marshall's decision in Marbury, which established the extra-constitutional power of judicial review.

The first action by the elites was the Judiciary Act of 1789, passed by the same set of Federalist elites who wrote the Constitution.

In the first step, the elites who wrote Madison's constitution created the framework of judicial procedural rules.

Then, in the same year, in the second step, they enacted legislation to empower the elites on the Supreme Court.

The 1789 Act established the federal judiciary of the United States, under the authority of Article III, Section 1, which prescribed that the "judicial power of the United States, shall be vested in one supreme Court, and such inferior Courts" as Congress saw fit to establish.

The Act made no provision for the composition or procedures of any of the courts, nor any text on removal of judges, leaving these issues in the hands of the Federalists, who controlled Congress.

Senator William Maclay, a natural rights populist from Pennsylvania, wrote his in his journal at the time,

> It certainly is a vile law system, calculated for expense and with a design to draw by degrees all law business into the Federal courts.

Maclay's reference to expense expressed the view that common citizens would not be able to afford to seek justice under this legal system.

Brutus reiterated this sentiment. He wrote,

> the costs of the supreme court will be so great, as to put it out of the reach of the poor and middling class of citizens to contest a suit in it.

The judicial system, in other words, was designed from the get-go, to be the exclusive province of the wealthy elite, who had the money to pursue justice, and who would subsequently use that power to deprive common citizens of their property, as in the debt-lien system applied against common farmers.

During the debates on the Act, Madison cleverly played both sides of the aisle, as he would do with the Bill of Rights, which he opposed, until he did not oppose it, and the Sedition Act, which he supported, until his friend, Jefferson, became a target of the Federalist oppression.

Madison wrote, on September 14, 1789,

> The Judiciary Act is now under consideration. I view it as you do, as defective both in its general structure, and many of its particular regulations. The attachment of the Eastern members, the difficulty of substituting another plan, with the consent of those who agree in disliking the bill, the defect of time &c, will however prevent any radical alterations.

In other words, Madison acknowledged that the Federalists had political power to enact their defective plan, which Madison had created when he wrote Article III, 2 years earlier.

Following Madison, the elite Federalists feared the "excesses of popular government."

In substituting the British system for Jefferson's natural rights republic, the Federalists eliminated the rights of citizens to democratically influence in the judicial system.

George Mason, a natural rights populist from Virginia, wrote that "the judiciary of the United States is so constructed and extended as to absorb and destroy the judiciaries of the several States."

The intent of the Federalists was to destroy the sovereignty of the states, and replace it with a centralized, consolidated government that had a latent tendency to become a socialist centralized tyranny.

As Brutus wrote,

> the judiciary under this system will have a power which is above the legislative, and which indeed transcends any power before given to a judicial by any free government under heaven.

From the time of ratification of the Articles of Confederation, a persistent minority of Federalists argued that state courts must be eliminated. Elimination of the state courts was the intent of the Judiciary Act of 1801.

In a historical precursor to the anti-Trump movement, the Federalist hoped that their second action would prevent the nomination of Jefferson.

They almost succeeded.

On the last weekend of March, 1801, the natural rights populists in both Virginia and Pennsylvania called out the state militia, in preparation for a civil war with the Federalists, who were attempting to overthrow Jefferson's election.

Violence was averted at the very last moment, but the debates on the Judiciary Act of 1801 revealed starkly different ideologies between natural rights populists, and the natural aristocracy about the place of the judiciary within a constitutional system of government.

Brutus wrote,

> But the judges under this constitution will controul the legislature, for the supreme court are authorised in the last resort, to determine what is the extent of the powers of the Congress; they are to give the constitution an explanation, and there is no power above them to set aside their judgment… In short, they are independent of the people, of the legislature, and of every power under heaven. Men placed in this situation will generally soon feel themselves independent of heaven itself.

It is this machinery of government that the global socialists seek to inherit.

The machinery was justified in the minds of the Federalists because they alone possessed the moral quality of virtue. Obtaining total control over government decisions, in the minds of Democrat socialists, is justified because they possess a superior mental power to make decisions about citizen welfare, that are better than decisions made by common citizens.

In either the case of the natural aristocracy or Democrat socialism, legitimate authority does not flow from the consent of the governed.

The election of Jefferson, and the debates over the Judicial Act of 1801, demonstrated to Marshall the uncertain status of elite judicial supremacy.

Marshall's decision in Marbury permanently cemented the elite judicial tyranny as the Supreme Law of the Land.

However, the power of the Federal Courts's judicial review is not mentioned in the text of the Constitution.

In a precursor to the penumbra in Griswold, (1965), Marshall's decision in Marbury, (1803), is based upon an emanation that Marshall obtained from reading the Declaration, which is not mentioned in Madison's Constitution.

Not only did Marshall's decision eviscerate the state courts, it set the precedent that subjective, private, idiosyncratic opinions of the Court were sanctioned by whatever ideological majority happened to be sitting on the Court.

In the absence of strict construction of the text, opinions like Dred Scott can be overruled by future courts.

Any majority can say "what the law is."

At the time the Court says what the law is, all other agencies and branches of government must obey the Supreme Law of the land. The other branches of government have no recourse against the Court for misapplication of the text.

Under a new majority in some future Court, the law of the land is something else.
Alexander Hamilton promised, in Federalist # 78, that the duty and power of judicial review does not mean the judiciary is supreme over the Constitution.

In ignoring Hamilton's promise, Marshall wrote in Marbury,

> the framers of the constitution contemplated that the document would establish the rules for the authority of the courts, as well as of the legislature.

Marshall's core proposition in Marbury is the interpretive independence of the Court over the actions of other branches of government, an authority that Marshall said flowed from

Madison's institutional separation of powers of the various departments.

Marshall's conclusion it is that the legitimate power of courts to refuse to give effect to legislative acts that the courts find to be in violation the rule of law supplied by the Constitution.

Marshall ruled that the powers of the legislature are defined and limited. Those limitations are binding, or else "We the People" cannot establish limits on the agents of government.

Marshall then draws the conclusion that legislative acts, at both the state and Federal level, which violate the Constitution are void, as determined by the power of judicial review.

In a regime of judicial interpretive supremacy, impeachment of justices on the grounds that their decisions are arbitrary, and deliberately violate the Constitution, is not legally possible.

Under Marbury, the decisions of the Court are the Constitution. Impeachment of the justices is impossible because the justices are the Constitution. The justices are the Constitution, and the Constitution is the justices.

The power of the Supreme Court is undefined and unlimited, under Marbury.
The Federal judicial machinery is deployed against state courts, in protecting the property rights of the natural aristocracy, now evolved today to mean America's corporate elite.

Lochner v. New York, (1905), the Supreme Court held unconstitutional a New York state law that limited bakers to a ten-hour workday, on the grounds that the law interfered with the baker's freedom of contract.

The New York state legislature had sought to protect workers against exploitation and abuse by limiting working hours.

The Supreme Court ruled that the New York law violated the clause of the Fourteenth Amendment that forbids any state from depriving anyone of life, liberty, or property, without due process of law.

Citing an individual right to "freedom of contract" purportedly implied by the Due Process Clause of the Fourteenth Amendment, the justices struck down the law as an unconstitutional interference by the state in private contractual relations between employers and employees.

As the Court did in both Dred Scott and Plessey, the Supreme Court claimed to be protecting the minority rights of the wealthy, against the tyranny of the democratic majority.

In his dissent, Oliver Wendell Holmes said, "The 14th Amendment does not enact Mr. Herbert Spencer's Social Statics."

From a strict construction of the text, the Constitution's commerce clause grants Congress no general control over the economy, nor does the 14th Amendment grant the Supreme Court authority over states, in economic policy.

Because of Marshall's extra-constitutional ruling in Marbury, Lochner became the Supreme Law of the Land, and citizens in New York had no recourse against the usurpation of their rights.

Socialism, by definition consists of the centralized direction of the economy, with government control over the means of production.

The centralized decisions of a socialist political elite determine both what will be produced and how the production will be distributed to citizens.

The Marxist ideology is based upon mental fantasies that the left constructs about the goodness of social justice and fairness.

In their social construction of reality, they create an economic image called, "forces of production." The "forces of production" produce goods and services, not individuals.

According to Marx, in the capitalist economy, the forces of production exploit the value of production produced by the collectivist entity group, "workers."

In all of history, and for all of time, in their mental fantasy, there are only two collectivist groups, the workers and the capitalists.

In socialism, the entire dynamic of economic history is the exploitation of workers by the capitalist class.

Marx preached the overthrow of the intricate economy of capitalism because it violated his moral values of fairness.

While Marx acknowledged that the capitalist system is the most productive economic system in history, he advocated a fundamental transformation of society that would place all of government decision making about production in the hands of a scientific elite, whose goal was social justice in the distribution of the production.

Obama believes exactly the same thing as Marx about the unfairness of the "capitalist" system.

Obama adds the moral principle that America is an evil empire because Madison's Constitution sanctioned slavery.

According to Obama, and the Democrat Party socialists, America can never overcome its original sin of slavery.

The goal for Obama, just like Marx, is the overthrow of the American capitalist economy, which is based upon private property, to a centralized economy, based upon government control of the means of production.

Consequently, the first step in overthrowing the economic system is gaining control of the American legal system that protects private property.

Obama's strategy for his attack is based upon a mental fantasy called "critical legal philosophy."

According to critical legal philosophy, America is so evil that it must be put under the yoke of a global economic system, and must not be allowed to continue as an independent sovereign nation.

There is nothing in Madison's judicial framework, or the power of Marshall's judicial review, that prohibits a socialist, like Obama, from deploying the centralized machinery of government to implement his locus of global sovereignty.

The end goal of the American judicial system, under Obama, is to replace national sovereignty with allegiance to international legal agencies. American legal and political agencies would enforce multilateral agreements and international law.

There is nothing philosophically incompatible between Madison's two social classes, the natural aristocracy and common citizens, and Marx's two social classes, the capitalist class and the workers.

There is nothing incompatible about global socialism between Obama's vision of globalism, and the goals of the modern day natural aristocracy of global corporations and global bankers, who manage the operations of "the swamp."

Under Madison's Constitution, sovereignty was relocated from the consent of the governed to the financial welfare of the natural aristocracy.

Under Obama, sovereignty is relocated from Madison's capitalist class to a global socialist elite, who manage global economic production and distribution.

Madison's amoral judicial machinery is functional under Obama's socialism because Marshall's decision in Marbury establishes a judicial elite tyranny that is not accountable to the consent of the governed.

Obama's two selections of socialist judges on the Supreme Court, continue the Democrat Party's precedent of substituting racial hatred for the equal application of the law.

Justice Sotomayor wrote, in the Michigan Affirmative Action case:

> The effect of this ruling is that a white graduate of a public Michigan university who whishes to pass his historical privilege on to his children may freely lobby the board of that university in favor of an expanded legacy admissions policy, whereas a black Michagander who was denied the opportunity to attend that very university cannot lobby the board in favor of a policy that might give his children a chance that he never had and that they might never have absent that policy.

There is nothing in the text of Madison's Constitution about historical white privilege.

But, Sotomayor's rulings, based upon her critical legal interpretation of America's racist past, are legitimate opinions, under Marshall's judicial review.

Sotomayor can make up the constitution as she goes along because Sotomayor is the Constitution, and the Constitution is whatever she says it is.

Because of Marshall's ruling, all the Democrats lack for implementing their socially constructed reality of centralized economic planning is the appointment of a socialist majority on the Supreme Court.

Natural rights are the rights God gives to every human being at his birth. Natural rights are inherent as an American birthright, and remain with the individual during life.

In America, an individual's natural rights cannot be separated or eliminated from his nature as a human being.

In contrast to God-given American natural rights, in socialism, rights inure to collectivist identity groups, and are granted by the government.

In the natural rights republic, individual liberty and justice, as the equal treatment of citizens in the law, are not separate moral values. Individual liberties are the natural rights that secure the sovereignty of the individual.

In socialism, justice as fairness in the pursuit of social justice, is more important than the pursuit of individual liberty. Justice, as fairness, is arbitrary and capricious because the judicial decisions are based upon a social construction of a reality that does not exist.

Madison's fundamental flaw is that his constitution did not secure individual liberty, and then, his judicial system allowed judges to pursue their idiosyncratic interpretation of the law, under Marshall's decision in Marbury.

In overcoming Madison's flaws, the Constitution of the Democratic Republic of America binds all judges to pursue the purpose of government:

> …that the National Government is instituted to allow individual citizens to pursue individual happiness and to limit the arbitrary application of government power over the lives of individuals……that the National Government is created by this union of states and the

> National Government shall never usurp the sovereign power or authority of the individual states or the sovereignty of the citizens in each state and that states have an inalienable right to call a convention of the states, without Congressional approval, to modify, amend, or abolish this Constitutional Contract.

Madison's original flaw was not to incorporate the British system of barriers to tyrannical judges in his constitution.

In a two-step sequence of events that compounded Madison's original flaw, both Judiciary Acts empowered a permanent judicial tyranny that is beyond the consent of the governed to remove judges.

Marshall's ruling in Marbury cemented the tyranny of the judicial system, ultimately leading to the centralized elite tyranny known today as "the swamp."

The Democratic Republic of America Constitution begins the process of correcting Madison's flaw by granting citizens a pathway to limit the power of judges.

All judges shall hold a term of office for six years, and may serve one additional term, if approved by the Senate.

No judge may serve more than two terms in a single court system, nor more than 18 years in both courts, in a lifetime.

The mandatory retirement age of all National judges is 70 years of age.

Madison's second flaw was to enable the Federal Courts unlimited scope of authority over both Federal law and all state laws.

The language in Madison's Constitution, and the subsequent ruling in Marbury, opened an unlimited scope of authority, while at the same time eviscerating the states as sovereign agents in the so-called "federalist system."

The Democratic Republic of America Constitution corrects this flaw with 3 provisions:

The judicial power of the National District and Supreme Courts extends to cases arising under the Constitution of the Democratic Republic of America.

A decision by the Supreme Court becomes the supreme law of the land for issues pertaining exclusively to the Constitution of the Democratic Republic of America.

> This Constitution, and the laws made by the National Congress, or which shall be made, under the Authority of the Democratic Republic, shall be the supreme Law of the Land for laws and cases exclusively pertaining to the National Government.

Madison's third flaw was his opposition to the Bill of Rights in his constitution because the written rights would ameliorate his intent of establishing unlimited authority of the Federal Government.

Madison opposed the Bill of Rights because he feared that the common citizens would oppress the wealthy minority by imposing taxes on the wealthy that could be paid in paper money issued by the states.

Madison said during the ratification debates that a Bill of Rights was not needed because the natural aristocracy possessed "virtue" and would never act to deny citizens their British common law rights.

Thanks to the radical egalitarian culture in North Carolina, citizens there refused to adopt Madison's constitution, until it contained a Bill of Rights.

The Federalists demonstrated their "virtue" by imposing economic sanctions on North Carolina, to coerce her citizens into joining the Union.

As a result of this clash, Madison agreed to incorporate a limited Bill of Rights.

The Constitution of the Democratic Republic corrects Madison's oversight by detailing a comprehensive set of rights of citizens:

- No citizen in any state shall be seized or imprisoned, or stripped of his rights or possessions, or outlawed or exiled, or deprived of his standing in any other way, nor shall agents of the government proceed with force against him, or send others to do so, except by the lawful judgment of a true bill of indictment by a majority vote of a grand jury of 18 citizens, or by the rules of judicial civil procedure of the National Government.
- No warrants or judicial orders in any criminal investigation shall be issued by a national court, except upon probable cause, determined in a judicial hearing, supported by an oath or affirmation of the government agent describing the specific items or locations to be searched and a judicial description of the crime being investigated.
- No person shall be held to answer for a capital, or otherwise infamous crime, unless on a presentment or indictment of a majority vote of a Grand Jury of 18 citizens who conduct an inquiry into the legitimacy of the government's allegation of a national crime.
- No citizen shall be subject for the same offence to be twice put in jeopardy of life or limb; nor shall be compelled in any criminal case to be a witness against himself.
- That all citizens are due the equal application of justice and that no citizen is entitled to special or unequal treatment of the application of the law.
- That all citizens are judged innocent until proven guilty in a trial of due process.
- In all criminal prosecutions, the accused shall enjoy the right to a speedy and public trial, by an impartial jury of the State and district wherein the

crime shall have been committed, which district shall have been previously ascertained by law, and to be informed of the nature and cause of the accusation; to be confronted with the witnesses against him; to have compulsory process for obtaining witnesses in his favor, and to have the assistance of counsel for his defense.
- The right of trial by jury shall be preserved, and no fact tried by a jury, shall be otherwise re-examined in any Court of the Democratic Republic of America, than according to the rules of the common law then obtaining in the national judiciary.
- Excessive bail shall not be required, nor excessive fines imposed, nor cruel and unusual punishments inflicted, nor imprisonment for longer than 5 days, in the absence of specific charges and allegation of crime.

Madison's fourth flaw was his deliberate omission of the British check against tyrannical judges. The Constitution of the Democratic Republic corrects Madison's mistake with the empowerment of a Citizens Grand Jury that provides citizen oversight on the judicial system.

- "...that a citizens Grand Jury of 18 citizens is impaneled, in each judicial district, for a term of 12 months, to protect and preserve the rights of citizens against the arbitrary application of government power against citizens..."
- That citizens have a civil right of action against elected representatives or agents of the National Government, for violation of these natural rights, upon a presentation of a motion of grievance to a Grand Jury of 18 citizens, who shall hear the case and determine the outcome and set the penalties for the violation by a majority vote.
- The a citizens Grand Jury in any State retains the right of initiating a citizen initiative on legislative proposals by a petition to the House of

Representatives, which must respond to the petition within 30 days of receipt.

Madison's Constitution relocated national "sovereignty" by making two changes in the Articles of Confederation. These two changes fundamentally altered the machinery of the American government from a natural rights republic to a British social class mixed government.

The National Judiciary of the Democratic Republic of America corrects Madison's flawed document by re-connecting the judicial system to Jefferson's Natural Rights Republic, and re-establishes the principle that all legitimate authority flows from the consent of the governed.

Chapter 4.
The Political Party and Election Rules of the Democratic Republic of America.

In his transformation of the American constitution from a natural rights republic, based on Jefferson's Declaration, to the British social class mixed government, Madison had to modify the British political party system to fit his vision of rule by the virtuous natural aristocracy.

The British political system is based upon a multi-party parliamentary system of proportional representation. The British political parties compete for votes, based upon their expression of how their party will serve the national public purpose of the United Kingdom.

The political party that promotes the most popular version of Res Publica wins a plurality of elected representatives, and that political party gets to form the new British government.

As he did in failing to adopt the entire British judicial system, Madison also failed to incorporate key elements of the British parliamentary system into his new constitutional rules.

His omission locked the U. S. political system into a dead-end, permanent, two-party system that eventually devolved into an unelected elite tyranny, called the swamp.

The reason that Madison failed to state his vision of Res Publica in the constitution is that his system of politics was based upon social class competition between the natural aristocracy and the common citizens, not on the pursuit of the American Res Publica.

"Res Publica" is the term used to describe the common cultural values that bind citizens into a national republic. A shared Res Publica is essential for creating the conditions of voluntary citizen obedience to the rule of law.

John Adams explained America's first Res Publica of liberty as a "public spiritedness as the only Foundation of the Republic."

Adams said,

> There must be a positive Passion for the public good…established in the Minds of the People, or there can be no Republican Government, nor any real liberty… Men must be ready, they must pride themselves, and be happy to sacrifice their private Pleasure, Passions and Interest.

Madison substituted class competition between the elites and common citizens for Jefferson's Res Publica.

As a historical outcome of Madison's flaw, the Democrat socialists today share no common cultural values with other American citizens.

Translating the citizen's consent of the governed into a public purpose of liberty was not relevant to Madison. Consequently, Madison's system of elected representation left out a political party that defended and protected the natural rights of citizens.

As President John Adams wrote in a letter to Benjamin Stoddert, the two political parties that had come into existence had defined financial ends, not the Res Publica of America.

"The reason," noted Adams,

> is that we have no Americans in America. The Federalistists have been no more Americans than the anties…Jefferson had a party. Hamilton had a party, but the commonwealth had none.

In other words, under Madison's class conflict model of government, liberty would have required its own political party. Liberty would be seen as just another special interest, like the financial interests of the natural aristocracy.

For example, the reason that the Republican Party never pushed back against Obama's transformation of America into a global socialist state is that Madison's constitution did not require Republicans to defend liberty.

Under Madison's two-class political system, the Republicans were only required to translate the political desires of the wealthy class into social and political policy, not to protect the citizen's loss of fundamental natural rights to a totalitarian socialist ideology.

Over time, the corrupt special interest political system, called "the spoils" system, led the Republicans to collaborate with the Democrats in keeping the special interest gravy train on track.

Both parties agreed that the spoils system was ultimately essential to making the political system work, for them. They both agreed that whoever won an election, that the winner could distribute the spoils to their special interests.

In their collaboration, there is nothing incompatible between the socialist vision of global socialism, and the Republican vision of a global corporate oligarchy.

The collaboration works well, as long as it is the Republican corporate elite who make the global economic rules that direct the global financial rewards to themselves.

What is new in American politics is the compatibility between the goals of global socialism of Democrats, and the goals of Republicans in promoting global corporatism.

Under Madison, there is no political party that protects the sovereignty of the citizens, or the sovereignty of the nation, from a globalist ideology.

What has changed in American politics is that the Democrats have abandoned their historical role of protecting the social class interests of common citizens, at the same time that Republicans have abandoned American sovereignty.

What is different today is that neither of the political parties derive their authority from the consent of the governed because the deep state agents who operate and manage the swamp owe their allegiance to the global elites, not to the Res Publica of America.

As explained by Merrill Jensen, in his book, Articles of Confederation, what the anti-federalistist did not realize, upon the ratification of the Articles of Confederation in 1781, was that the Federalists intended to overthrow the natural rights republic.

In his review of Hamilton's Federalist Papers, Richard Bernstein posed the basic political question addressed by Madison and Hamilton:

> Was it dangerous in a democratic government, to have important officers insulated from control by the people, or was it necessary to accept that risk in order to protect fundamental rights from infringement by popular passions or political intrigue?

Madison understood, according to Marvin Meyers, in The Mind of the Founder, that man was a "social" animal moved by self-interest.

His dilemma was how to re-write the rules so that,

> ...self-interested, self-governing men would be obliged to respect the rights of others and serve the permanent and aggregate interests of the community.

Madison solved his dilemma by excluding the "howling masses" from the government, because the common citizens lacked "virtue."

As Stuart Hill notes in Democratic Values and Technological Choice, Madison's main concern was "...how one faction would use political power to oppress another group."

The key concern of Madison was that the majority of common citizens would form a political party that would oppress the minority of wealthy elites. Madison called this outcome "tyranny."

The solution, for Madison, was permanently loading the constitutional deck against common citizens.

The true distinction of the American system, wrote Madison in Federalist #71, "lies in the total exclusion of the people, in their collective capacity in any share in the government."

Madison shared the opinion of Jonathan Jackson that the main threat of tyranny originated in the excesses of democracy at the state level.

In his 1788 book, Thoughts Upon The Political Situation in the United States, Jackson wrote,

> A natural aristocracy that had to dominate public authority in order to prevent America from degenerating into a democratic licentiousness, into a government where the people would be directed by no rule but their own will and caprice...Tyranny by the people was the worst kind because it left few resources to the oppressed (the elites).

In The Natural Rights Republic, Michael Zuckert calls Madison's constitutional rules "institutional instrumentalism."

This description means that Madison created the institutional rules that are instrumental in effecting the distribution of power in the republic permanently to the natural aristocracy.

For Madison, the purpose of government is not to provide a mechanism of rights claims and reciprocation of trust.

Rather, Madison's rules were the instruments to balance and check factional political power in order to insure that social elites, the natural leaders, who made important decisions on behalf of all society, were insulated from the tyranny that could be imposed by the people.

In The Articles of Confederation, Jensen writes,

> ...the federalists adopted a theory of the sovereignty of the people, in the name of the people, and erected a federalist government whose purpose was to thwart the will of the people in whose name they acted...

In turn, Jensen explains that what the federalists failed to see, in 1787, was that the government that they had created could be captured by the socialists, in 2008.

As Gordon Wood has pointed out, in The Creation of the American Republic, not only did Madison's scheme provide for a system dominated by

> ...natural leaders who knew better than the people as a whole what was good for society," but it also succeeded in removing the non-natural leaders from the political process.

Wood noted,

> In fact, the people did not actually participate in government any more...The American (Federalists) had taken the people out of the government altogether.

Gouverneur Morris, a Federalist elite from New York, who strangely represented Pennsylvania at the Convention, stated in 1774, that the British connection was the guarantee of the existing aristocratic order...after the revolution, they engaged with Federalists in other states in undoing the Articles of Confederation.

As the natural rights populist, Centinel, asked about Madison's arrangement, "If the people are sovereign how does the opinion of citizens direct the policies of government?"

There is nothing in the Federalist constitution, noted Centinel, like the detailed definition of consent of citizens, as in the various state constitutions.

Or, he could have added, like the safeguards against tyranny in the British political system.

As Sean Wilentz wrote, in The Rise of American Democracy,

> The people had no formal voice of their own in government. And, that was exactly how it was supposed to be – for once the electors had chosen their representatives, they ceded power, reserving none for themselves until the next election...The people, as a political entity, existed only on election day.

As a result of this constitutional orientation, the role of the federalist government in economic policy matters became skewed towards issues like making certain that the bondholders of federalist debt were repaid at full face value for the bonds they had bought for pennies on the dollar.

As Elisha Douglass noted, in Rebels and Democrats,

> Hence, a double paradox: to preserve their own liberty, the unprivileged masses must be prevented from infringing on the privileged few; to maintain a government based on consent, a large proportion of the

people must be deprived of the ability to extend or withhold consent.

At a 1792 dinner party in New York, with Federalists, William Maclay, a U. S. Senator from Pennsylvania, was astonished at the bold, loud, boisterous elites bragging that they had pulled a fast one over the non-elites.

Maclay wrote,

> the Federalists at the dinner party were boasting that they had "cheated the People" and established a form of Government over the people which none of them expected.

"Cheating the people" was the intent of Madison's two-party political system, that permanently damaged the natural rights of citizens.

Madison's political logic was empowered by the logic of his two-party, two class, political competition, where no one, or no political party, represented the Res Publica of the new nation.

In his Second Treatise of Government, Locke identified the basis of a legitimate government.

According to Locke, a ruler gains authority through the consent of the governed. The elected leaders gain consent through the political system, like the one in Britain, that features competition among political parties for the most popular version of Res Publica.

The duty of that government is to protect the natural rights of the people, which Locke believed to include life, liberty, and property.

Locke wrote that if the government should fail to protect these rights, its citizens would have the right to overthrow that government.

In contrast to Locke's consent of the governed, the Democrat socialists today have a different interpretation of the function of government.

Jim Newell, a Democrat socialist writer from Slate, writes,

> Among wide swaths of the Democratic coalition, there is an orthodoxy forming: The party's purpose is to block and resist Trump at every turn, and "through that process reinforce their own (socialist) priorities.

Rather than consent of the governed, the Democrat's philosophy is to "reinforce" their cultural values in extra-legal political action, called "resistance."

Their goal is a totalitarian state that enforces socialist collectivist values, with an unelected propagandist, like Newell, as an elite leader of the socialist regime.

The logic of resistance is enabled by Madison's flaw in embedding the two party political system.

In the absence of Res Publica, Madison's "first-past-the-post, winner-take-all special interest corruption model, empowers the Democrats to override the will of the citizens.

In Madison's first past the post model, one political party receives a majority of the vote, and that party gets to form the new government. In the winner-take-all system of electing candidates to office, the losers have a very limited role in governing.

In many cases in the U. S. political history, the rules enable a candidate with less than a majority to win an election.

For example, Abraham Lincoln won the presidency in 1860 even though he clearly lacked majority support, given the number of candidates in the race.

In 1860, four candidates competed for the presidency: Lincoln, a Republican; two Democrats, one from the northern wing of the party and one from the southern wing; and a member of the newly formed Constitutional Union Party, a southern party that wished to prevent the nation from dividing over the issue of slavery.

Votes were split among all four parties, and following Madison's rules, a minority candidate lead the nation into the Civil War, whose genesis lay in the unresolved rules about slavery, in Madison's constitution.

The logic of Madison's political system for elections derives from his famous 3/5 compromise of June 11, 1787.

The 3/5 clause empowered southern slave states with 60% greater representation in the Electoral College, and while slavery has been outlawed, the legacy of slavery lives on in Madison's election rules, in his flawed Constitution.

Madison's idea for implementing the British social class political system was to create a U. S. Senate that functioned like the British House of Lords, and have a President that functioned like the British king.

Madison supported the resolution of John Dickson, a federalist delegate from Delaware, on the creation of the Senate.

Dickson's resolution stated that,

> we ought to carry it through such a refining process as will assimilate it as near as may be to the House of Lords in England.

Madison realized that it had been their connection with British nobility, prior to the Revolution, that had granted them their privileged status to run their colonies, and to speculate in lands and war bonds.

Madison presumed that the minority of wealthy elites would win elections because of the way he wrote the rules.

First past the post was the logic of his system that ensured ongoing elite political control. First-past-the-post was aided and abetted by the 3/5 clause.

As Madison admitted, in his 1792 essay, A Candid State of Parties, "...some of the supporters of the Constitution are openly or secretly attached to monarchy and aristocracy."

As he noted, the Federalists had,

> debauched themselves into a persuasion that mankind are incapable of governing themselves, and believed that government can only be carried on by the pageantry of rank, the influence of money and emoluments, and the terror of military force.

As he so often did in his life, Madison played both sides of his argument. First, in 1787, he adopted the British class system in his constitution that served to empower the elites.

Next, in 1792, he criticized his own work because it created a political system based upon the influence of money.

Madison used the ancient legal definition of rights as a grant of legal title of ownership from the King, or the Church, or some other powerful authority, to some group, like the Lords, or the commoners, or capitalists.

The Democrat party socialists extend Madison's concept of rights to mean that the elites in government grant rights to collectivist entities, who share grievances against the capitalist class.

In contrast to rights granted by the King, Jefferson and Locke wrote that natural rights are granted by God.

Madison's frequent use of the term "faction" in the Federalist Papers to describe a social class is compatible with his collective expression of "the people" to describe where he thought the greatest danger to the stability of the republic lay.

"We the people" is a collectivist entity that is easily adapted to the socialist ideology of identity group interests.

The aristocratic American government created by Madison was stable as long as the Republicans (the well born), created economic growth.

After 1992, when the American economy no longer experienced economic growth, citizens became susceptible to the propaganda of socialism.

In Federalist Paper #57, Madison and Hamilton wrote that the most important barriers to the elevation of traitors to the public liberty were frequent elections and a "limitation of the term of appointments."

Madison first promised that his system was based upon frequent elections and term limits. He then implemented the exact opposite system that featured no term limits for elected representatives and life-time tenure for Federalist judges.

If both political parties share a united federalist culture of values of perpetuating the spoils system, and if the elites can control the election apparatus in each district, with no fear of term limits, it does not matter from which district the elite is elected.

Once the elected representative arrives in Washington, D.C., the federalist values of the special interest spoils are all the same.

In America's current two party special interest environment, the political elites are not bound by the same rules that are imposed upon the non-elites, and not subjected to feelings of cultural value disloyalty when they manipulate the rules for their own advantage.

Madison presumed that the Federalist representatives obtained the consent of the citizens in the original constitutional grant, of 1789, and then, after that, the common citizens granted the elites the authority to make all the decisions.

Madison's arrangement leaves citizens vulnerable to the tyranny of socialism, because the socialists will use the first past the post two party political mechanisms created by Madison to obtain power, and then use his constitutional institutional arrangement to never relinquish power.

Madison's flawed constitution contains no remedy for this outcome.

The "Mob-rule" of Democrat resistance in the swamp, and the ensuing civil disorder, is the consequence of the American constitution that was written to eliminate the consent of the governed.

On September 15, 1787, on the day Madison's constitution was published, George Mason stated that the plan was exceptionable and dangerous.

Mason stated,

> As the proposing of amendments (in Article 5), is in both modes to depend in the first immediately and in the second ultimately on Congress, no amendments of the proper kind would ever be obtained by the people, if the Government should become oppressive.

Mason went on to say that Americans had been duly warned about the incipient aristocratic tyranny resulting from the work of the 37 elites who drafted the document, in secret.

Recent historical scholarship documents that two elites, on the very last days of the convention, hijacked the document, in a "Committee of Detail," to imbed changes that had never been debated or seen before, by the other delegates.

Mason described the subterfuge of these two delegates,

> These gentlemen who will be elected senators, will fix themselves in the federalist town, and become citizens of that town more than of your state. This government will commence in a moderate aristocracy,

Mason added,

> It is at present impossible to foresee whether it will, in its operation, produce a monarchy or a corrupt, oppressive aristocracy, it will most probably vitiate some years between the two, and then terminate in the one or the other.

Mason, and the other natural rights populists, mis-named as anti-federalistists, clearly forecast the creation of the modern swamp in D. C.

The so-called representative republic of Madison ended in 2008, in a corrupt, oppressive aristocracy, with an incipient potential for a socialist totalitarian state.

When Madison adopted part of the British class system, he truncated it to better fit the new American experience. Without the Res Publica of the British experience that limits tyranny, citizens in America do not have political vehicles to translate their values into political policy.

Under Madison's flawed, truncated, two-party arrangement, given the absence of constitutional Res Publica, natural rights conservatives have no alternative, except to vote for candidates of the Republican Party.

The government that Madison overthrew, in 1787, was the voluntary economy of exchange of the Articles of Confederation, where common citizens could freely gain the value of their labor (property).

Madison replaced the Articles, based upon equal commercial exchanges, with government rules, where the elites dominated the terms of financial exchange with their unbalanced, and unchecked government power.

Their government power included a distorted federalist judicial system, erecting barriers to ballot access, campaign financing hurdles for non-elites, gerrymandering, exclusion from debates of minority parties, voter fraud, and media propaganda.

The consequence of Madison's flawed arrangement is neither a representative republic based upon the rule of law nor a system of government, based on the on the natural rights of the consent of the governed.

As it does in usurping the sovereign power of state courts, the Federalist Government has steadily eroded state political rights to control their own election laws.

The Supreme Court ruled in 1964 that both houses of all state legislatures had to be based on election districts that were relatively equal in population size, under the "one man, one vote" principle.

The Supreme Court appointed itself as judge of the election districts.

In 1972, the Court ruled that state legislatures had to redistrict every ten years based on census results. Agents of the Federalist government assumed unelected authority to pass judgment on the new districts.

Four of the fifteen post-Civil War constitutional amendments were ratified to extend Federalist jurisdiction over the voting rights of different groups of citizens. These extensions state that voting rights cannot be denied or abridged based on the following:

- Race, color, or previous condition of servitude" (15th Amendment, 1870).
- On account of sex. (19th Amendment, 1920).
- By reason of failure to pay any poll tax or other tax" for federalist elections (24th Amendment, 1964).
- Citizens who are eighteen years of age or older, shall not be denied or abridged by the United States or by any state on account of age" (26th Amendment, 1971).

In his reinterpretation of Locke and Jefferson, Madison assumed that the citizens agreed that the purpose of the government was to provide the initial consent to establish rules governing property rights and financial exchange.

Madison, and the 37 elites assembled in Philadelphia, assumed that market exchange relationships, based upon the right of private property, required the centralized power of the Federalist government to enforce the orderly mechanisms of exchange that would be uniform in all the states.

After the citizens provided this initial consent, their on-going consent of the governed would never be required again.

The government that Madison created served the needs of the special class interests of the natural aristocracy.

That group's preferences become the surrogate national social welfare function of the new nation.

Under Obama, the government serves a unified socialist ideology. In economic terms, the national social welfare that was maximized, under Obama, served the interests of their global socialist religion.

The term "We the People" serves the same purpose under Obama's socialism, as the term serves in Article 2 of the Soviet Constitution of 1977, "the people (we the people), exercise state power through the vanguard Communist Party."

In the soviet communist constitution of 1977, the expression of popular sovereignty was described as the unity of state power to achieve the highest welfare for all the citizens.

Under Obama, the Democrat Party becomes the vanguard political party, just like the Communist Party in Russia.

As a consequence of Madison's two-party political arrangement, American society is equally divided between 65 million socialist voters who voted for Hillary, and the 63 million natural rights conservatives voters, who elected Donald Trump.

The Res Publica of natural rights and liberty of the 63 million voters who voted for Trump, cannot be reconciled with the Res Publica of the 65 million socialists who voted for the cause of global socialism.

The two values, individual liberty and collectivist social justice, are irreconcilably opposed and cannot co-exist.

Madison's constitutional arrangement was designed to check and balance the social class interests of the few over the many, not to check and balance socialism versus freedom.

In 2008, when both political parties failed to fulfill their historical class purposes, citizens were left with no form of representation of their natural and civil rights.

The allegiance to the rule of law in a natural rights republic is rooted in shared cultural customs and traditions of family, church, and community. The bonds of loyalty between citizens are strengthened when citizens join each other in common endeavors, like membership in a church.

As the shared cultural values are strengthened, voluntary obedience to the rule of law increases.

The civic associations, trade guilds, churches, and professional groups in America all have articles of incorporation and by-laws based upon ethical codes of behavior for their members.

These type of ethical codes and moral values are the same that undergird voluntary obedience to the rule of law when citizens form their new government, and leave the state of nature.

The civic clubs are self-governing, meaning that they enforce their own laws and rules upon their members, without calling upon the police power of the state. This is like the on-going consent that citizens agree to, after the new government has been formed.

The pluralism of multiple civic clubs in America functions to connect citizens to each other, and to bind them to a common set of national moral values, within their local communities.

The clubs function to provide the social institutional mechanism of social reciprocity because the members of each club agree to discharge their duties to other members, in the same way that citizens agree to discharge their duty to defend the other citizen's natural rights.

It is an easy transition for citizens to apply their lessons and experience in managing their civic and community clubs to managing their affairs in government. The local community and civic groups provided the bonds of affiliation with other citizens.

The shared cultural values of natural rights is the basis of the natural rights constitution. Equality in natural rights leads to a constitution based upon majority rule.

Majority rule is the means to implement a government based upon the principle of equal rights of all, and special privileges for none.

Allegiance to the rule of law is promoted by citizens who have consented to make decisions by majority rule in their constitution.
Jefferson called this idea "self-government."

In the Democratic Republic of America, political parties act as the mediating forum in the relationship between individual citizens, and the institutional structure of government.

The political parties act as the mechanism through which cultural values are transmitted to elected representatives into laws and rules.

The parties represent the connection between the practical knowledge of how government works and the cultural values of society.

The parties answer Centinel's question about the obvious flaw in Madison's constitution about translating the will of the citizens into law.

In other words, there exists a public purpose in a having a fair political process, wherein citizens meet to make informed decisions, that is independent of the partisan fortunes of any particular political party or elected official.

The translation of the will of the citizens into laws, through voting on representatives, requires the police protection of the state to insure the integrity of the process.

How votes are cast and counted, and how votes are authenticated is too important a civic function to leave to the private special interests of partisan parties, as it currently exists today, in the swamp.

The mechanics of the voting process would be separated from the partisan interests of political parties in determining the outcome of the voting.

The institution of government is conceived as a generic extension of the will of the citizens, and not as an independent arbitrator of special interest greed.

One of the key differences in viewing the institution of government as part of the will of citizens is to overcome one of Hamilton's flaws that political transactions are just like economic transactions, and that by extension, government is like a private business.

Obama's socialist transformation replaced the pluralism of multiple civic clubs with a unified, totalitarian cultural value of global socialism.

The purpose and intent of Obama's relentless socialist propaganda media is to have citizens express loyalty and allegiance to the federalist government, as if the federalist government were functioning in the same capacity of creating citizen affiliations as the local community groups.

Madison's Constitution did not address the issue of political parties because Madison assumed that the elites would always be the ruling class.

Madison did not want political parties to be formed because they would result in the majority party of common citizens exploiting the financial interests of the wealthy minority.

Madison's term for political parties was "faction." Madison's term for majority exploitation was "tyranny."

In the absence of constitutional Res Publica, Madison's political rules devolved into the spoils system, where election winners rewarded the campaign contributors with lucrative government jobs and government contracts.

In the earlier era, the spoils system was loosely linked to the election system. What changed in America is that the spoils system, managed by the swamp, is no longer connected to the consent of the governed.

The global elites obtain their spoils without the burden of obtaining citizen consent.

The constitutional framework of the Democratic Republic of America returns government to Jefferson's principles of "self-government," based upon the political equality of all citizens.

The Democratic Republic Constitution strictly limits the domain of government power from infringing on the freedom and liberty of citizens to re-establish the primacy of civic associations, expressed in Jefferson's Declaration.

Elections and the regulation of political parties in the Democratic Republic is based upon 4 fundamental principles:

- **Fair Rules for National Elections.**
- **Fair Rules on the Function and Authority of the National Government.**
- **Fair Rules for Political Parties.**
- **Fair and Competitive Elections**

Fair Rules for National Elections.

The Constitution establishes procedures for voter qualifications and voting procedures, in national elections.

The Constitution requires elected representatives to swear an oath of allegiance to defend the constitution and the rights of citizens, as expressed in the Declaration of Independence.

Fair Rules on the Function and Authority of the National Government.

The Constitution establishes term limits of all elected representatives.

Senators serve four year terms and may succeed in office once, and no more than 10 years in a lifetime.

All House of Representatives serve two year terms, and no more than 4 terms total and no more than 10 years in a lifetime.

The Constitution of the Democratic Republic of America returns to the rule of electing one U. S. Senator, per state, whose constitutional mission is to protect the interests of citizens in their states from the threat of tyranny of the central government.

The Constitution establishes term limits of 10 years for all government employees and congressional staff.

The Constitution establishes a bright line rule for impeachment of elected federalist representatives, or appointed officials, initiated by either the national government, or in the legislatures of the states.

The Constitution establishes restrictions of the domain of power of the National Bank and national treasury to policies which inure to the exclusive benefit of U. S. citizens and to the benefit of the sovereign U. S. domestic economy.

The Constitution establishes limits on the issuance of national debt and a constitutional requirement that the U. S. Department of the Treasury limit the national debt ceiling to a target debt level in any 10 year period, by approval of a majority of state legislatures.

The Constitution limits the National Congress to laws "expressly" enumerated in the Constitution that defend natural rights from the non-elected agents of government.

The Constitution requires that each law passed by the National Congress contain a preamble that justifies the enactment as necessary and proper to the defense of natural rights and the sovereignty of the Nation.

The Constitution mandates that before any law be made for raising taxes, the purpose for which any tax is to be raised will appear clearly to the preamble of the legislation stating the constitutional integrity of the tax.

For example, any revenue or tax bill would contain a preamble as styled:

"That the people have a right to uniform government; and, therefore, that no bill or tax whose interests are outside the sovereign interests of the United States, or separate from, or independent of the government of the United States, ought to be enacted."

Fair Rules for Political Parties.

The Constitution establishes the right of citizens in each state to recall nationally elected representatives by vote of the registered members of the parties that elected the elected representative.

The Constitution sets time limits between campaign announcements and elections. Parties select candidates for office in August for national election held in last weekend of October.

Voter ID cards are issued by the state Secretary of States. ID cards, along with other identification must be presented by a voter, at the voting booth.

Candidates running for office must clearly state in all public announcements their party affiliation, and that if elected, they will support their party platform.

Six weeks before a national election, a political party must publish their party platform and state how the platform supports the Res Publica of natural rights.

Fair and Competitive Elections.

The Constitution establishes House election districts by quantitative criteria, for periods of 10 years.

The Constitution delegates power to each State Secretary of State the authority to form state election commissions to oversee integrity of voter registration and voting process in each federalist election

Candidates for each party swear and affirm an oath to defend the stated principles of the party, if elected.

Political parties are registered by State Secretary of State, as non-profit corporations.

New political parties are certified by State Secretary of State by valid petition signed by registered members of the party equal to 10% of all registered voters in the state.

Parties are de-certified by Secretary of State in any national presidential election where the total votes cast by registered members for President is less than 10%.

Secretary of State issues voter ID card for all non-affiliated registered voters.

Multiple political parties compete for votes, and the party obtaining the plurality gets to form the new government.

Conclusion.

When the state delegates from Mecklinburg County were sent to North Carolina's first state constitutional convention, in 1776, the citizens who elected them gave the delegates specific instructions.

According to Charles Maddry, in The North Carolina Constitution of 1776,

> The delegates were instructed to endeavor to establish a free government under the authority of the people of North Carolina – a simple democracy, the fundamental principles of which should oppose everything leaning toward autocracy or power in the hands of the rich against the poor.

The political party and election rules of the Democratic Republic of America re-claim those North Carolina principles of 1776, by implementing a political system based upon the Res Publica of the liberty of citizens, and not on Madison's system of political spoils.

Chapter 5.
The Restoration of State Sovereignty In the Democratic Republic of America.

"We the People" is the single most damaging text of Madison's Constitution, in terms of damaging state sovereignty and individual natural rights.

The text has been used by the U. S. Supreme Court, for 230 years, as the justification for the Federalist conversion of the American government from a natural rights individualistic culture of individual states, to a centralized, consolidated national government.

The charade of "We the People" hides the fact that there were no "We the People," who wrote the Constitution.

There were only 37 self-appointed, self-selected, financial elites who signed an unbalanced, unfair set of rules that empowered the elites with perpetual control over non-elites.

Madison called for the Grand Convention in a resolution to the Virginia Legislature. Only 6 states responded to Madison's call to amend the Articles of Confederation.

The six states formed a phantom shadow government, called the "Confederation Congress" to manage the affairs of the convention.

Six states refused to respond to Madison's resolution because they wanted the authentic, real, national Congress created by the Articles, to authorize the convention.

Madison's shadow government issued a resolution that the delegates would meet in May of 1787, in Philadelphia, for the sole, exclusive purpose of amending the Articles of Confederation.

Madison wrote the resolution, which stated:

> A Convention of delegates should meet for the sole purpose of revising the articles of Confederation and reporting to Congress and the several legislatures such alterations and provisions therein as shall, when agreed to in Congress and confirmed by the States, render the federal Constitution adequate to the exigencies of government and the preservation of the Union.

Madison knew that "amending" the Articles was a lie when he wrote the resolution.

"We the People" is a collectivist description of a myth that the entire population sat down together, and agreed to form a more perfect union.

It is not based upon individual natural rights, and the text can easily be adopted by the socialist Democrats today to justify imposing their form of totalitarian collectivism on non-socialists.

The 37 elites who signed the Constitution are no more "We the People," than a minority of socialists who claim today to be "We the People."

Among the so called "Founding Fathers," there was not one representative of the common citizens.

No farmers, no tradesmen, no small merchants. Just wealthy northern bankers, and southern plantation slave-owners.

In the last days of the Convention, a single person, Gouverneur Morris, a wealthy elite from New York, converted the original text in the Preamble, "We the People of the individual United States," followed by a detailed listing of the 13 states, to "We the People of the United States, omitting all reference to the states entirely.

The 37 elites who signed the Constitution on September 17, 1787, had not seen the change made by Morris, before they saw the document, for the first time, on September 12.

Morris made his change in the text on September 11, 1787. His change, and the entire document, was presented to the delegates on September 12, 1787.

Before Morris made his secret change in the text, the parties to the new contract would have been the governments of the individual states, and a new national government.

The text in the Preamble would have been just like the text in the Articles of Confederation, before Morris made his secret change.

The legal entity being created would have been a confederation of states, who agreed to delegate limited powers to the new Federal government.

After Morris made his change, the parties to the contract were a collectivist, synthetic, mythical entity, "We the People," and a single, consolidated national government, that operated directly on all "We the People."

All of the elites understood the implication of the change in converting the government from a confederation of states to a centralized national government that would assume the power of the "Supreme Law of the Land," over all the state governments and all the mythical "We the People."

There was no need for a public debate.

All the elites knew that they needed a centralized national government in order to gain supreme financial and legal control over the government, in order to be paid taxes and debt in gold and silver.

The entire process of appointing delegates to the Constitutional Convention was a fraud. The various states, either appointed delegates, or allowed the delegates to self-select themselves, to attend the Convention.

Initially, 73 delegates were appointed or selected by the 13 states.

The appointed delegates were given explicit instructions, from their state legislatures, that their mission in Philadelphia was to "amend" the existing Articles of Confederation.

But, amending the Articles was not Madison's intent. From the time he left the Annapolis Convention, in September of 1786, Madison was privately communicating his intent to overthrow the Articles of Confederation.

The cabal in Annapolis that hatched this secret plan consisted of 12 elites, from 5 states, all of whom agreed that the Articles must be abolished.

Of the original 73 delegates, 18 of the delegates learned of Madison's intent to implement a new government, and chose not to attend.

Of the original 73 delegates appointed, 55 attended the Convention, for limited durations.

The entire delegation of New York left Philadelphia, leaving a single representative, Alexander Hamilton, whose instructions from the state legislature forbid him from acting without the presence of the other delegates.

Hamilton proceeded to illegally sign the Constitution, on behalf of the entire state of New York.

Of the 55 delegates who attended, only 37 delegates signed the document.

George Mason, like many other natural rights patriots in opposition, simply left Philadelphia, and refused to sign it.

The document contained an illegal amendment to the Articles that required Madison's Constitution to be ratified by 9 states. "We the People" was actually "We the People," of only 9 states.

The entire ratification process was a fraud that evaded the legal authority of the 13 state governments, as required by the Articles.

The rigged ratification conventions included corruption and fraud, including the use of the police power of the State of Pennsylvania to coerce their state delegates to vote for the new constitution.

The rulings by the U. S. Supreme Court, that subordinated the sovereignty of state governments to the federal government, can best be understood when placed into the context of economic and financial interests of the elites.

"We the People" is continually deployed by the Supreme Court as the legal justification to protect and preserve the privileged political status of the elites to use the power of government for their own financial advantage.

The best historical analysis of the Constitution, and the ensuing 230 year history court rulings based upon "We the People," is Charles Beard's 1913 book, an Economic Interpretation of the Constitution.

Beard begins by making a distinction between personal financial assets and real estate assets.

The northern Founding Fathers were bankers and lawyers who needed the new Constitution to protect their personal assets, which included "money, public securities, manufactures, and trade and shipping."

The northerners were the protagonists in Philadelphia, and assumed an offensive posture in eliminating the Articles of Confederation.

Gouvenor Morris, who changed the text of the Preamble, was a northern financial elite.

The southern Founding Fathers needed to protect their real estate and slaves from northern depredations. The southerners were primarily in a defensive posture to limit northern financial interests from harming their southern way of life.

However, since the southern elite had bought the Revolutionary War bonds for pennies on the dollar, from destitute common farmer-soldiers, they had a common interest with the northern bankers in being paid their principal and interest in gold and silver, not the nearly worthless paper dollars issued by the state governments.

In other words the common point of collaboration between the northern and southern elites lay in eliminating the authority of state governments to issue paper money.

The authority of state governments would be replaced by a consolidated federal authority that would become the "Supreme Law of the Land," in order to compel citizens to pay their debts in gold and silver.

As Beard explained,

> The Constitution was an essentially economic document based upon the concept that the fundamental private rights of property are anterior to government and morally beyond the reach of popular majorities... A "large property-less mass was excluded from participation in all stages of the process... The Constitution was ratified by a vote of probably not more than one-sixth of the adult males... Put differently, the Constitution was created by and for "substantial property interests.

The Federalist elites possessed a false pride that they alone were smarter than the common herd, just like the socialists today, who claim to have a superior mental ability to make decisions on behalf of all citizens.

As Hamilton wrote in Federalist #1, the new constitution was,

> a unique event in the history of the world; finally government was going to be established by reflection and choice rather than force and fraud.

Subsequently, the Federalists engaged in force and fraud to ratify their new constitution that granted them perpetual power to make laws by their own reflection. The fraud included Hamilton's signing the document, without legal authority, on behalf of all of New York.

The job of the U. S. Supreme Court was to deploy the language in the Preamble to preserve the elite's privileged power.

Beginning in 1793, the Supreme Court began cementing the foundation of the consolidated, centralized national government that eviscerated the sovereignty of state governments, using the logic of "We the People.

In Chisholm v. Georgia, (1793), the first chief justice, John Jay wrote,

> In establishing the Constitution, the people exercised their own rights, and their own proper sovereignty, and conscious of the plenitude of it, they declared with becoming dignity, 'We the People of the United States, do ordain and establish this Constitution.' Here we see the people acting as sovereigns of the whole country; and in the language of sovereignty, establishing a Constitution by which it was their will, that the State Governments should be bound, and to which the State Constitutions should be made to conform. Every State Constitution is a compact made by and between the citizens of a State to govern themselves in a certain manner; and the Constitution of the United States is

likewise a compact made by the people of the United States to govern themselves as to general objects, in a certain manner.

Jay was born in December, 1745, into a wealthy family of New York merchants and government officials. It was politically imperative for him to use "We the People" as the mythical ruse that would allow his wealthy northern Federalists to solidify their position of privilege over the mythical synthetic mass of citizens, called "We the People."

He wrote,

> The Supreme Court has denied the assumption that full and unqualified sovereignty still remains in the states or the people of a state, and affirm[ed], on the contrary, that, by express words of the constitution, solemnly ratified by the people of the United States, the national government is supreme within the range of the powers delegated to it; while the states are sovereign only in the sense that they have an indisputable claim to the exercise of all the rights and powers guarantied to them by the constitution of the United States, or which are expressly or by fair implication reserved to them.

His logic is that "the people" in their capacity as individual citizens in the states are a different legal class than the "We the People" who agreed to form the new constitution.

When "We the People" citizens gave their initial consent to form the new constitution, the citizens in the states agreed to subordinate the sovereignty of their state governments to the federal government, forever.

In Marbury v Madison (1803), Chief Justice Marshall borrowed from the text of the Declaration, which was not in Madison's Constitution, in order to justify the principle of judicial review, an undelegated power not in the Constitution.

Marshall used a derivative of "We the People" by citing "The people," as the term appeared in the Declaration.

Marshall wrote,

> That the people have an original right to establish for their future government such principles as, in their opinion, shall most conduce to their own happiness is the basis on which the whole American fabric has been erected. The exercise of this original right is a very great exertion; nor can it nor ought it to be frequently repeated. The principles, therefore, so established are deemed fundamental. And as the authority from which they proceed, is supreme, and can seldom act, they are designed to be permanent.

Marshall's logic of his opinion hinges upon the idea that the synthetic, imaginary entity "the people," established the Constitution, following the logic of Morris in the Preamble. The grant of authority that "the people," gave to the Federal government was not from the states, but from "the people."

Marshall then connects the authority of the people to establish a constitution with the legal imperative that the original grant of authority established a "Supreme Law," for all of time immemorial. As Marshall noted, the grant of authority from the people "was designed to be permanent."

Marshall wrote,

> The Constitution is either a superior, paramount law, unchangeable by ordinary means, or it is on a level with ordinary legislative acts, and, like other acts, is alterable when the legislature shall please to alter it…It has been insisted at the bar, that, as the original grant of jurisdiction to the Supreme and inferior courts is general, and the clause assigning original jurisdiction to the Supreme Court contains no negative or restrictive words, the power remains to the Legislature to assign original jurisdiction to that Court in other

> cases than those specified in the article which has been recited, provided those cases belong to the judicial power of the United States.

After "We the People" established the government, according to Marshall, only the Supreme Court could interpret what the law was.

Marshall wrote,

> It is emphatically the province and duty of the Judicial Department to say what the law is. Those who apply the rule to particular cases must, of necessity, expound and interpret that rule. If two laws conflict with each other, the Courts must decide on the operation of each.

Marshall's opinion meant that only, and exclusively, the Supreme Court, henceforth, could say what the law was in all federal and state courts. His phrase "original grant of jurisdiction to the Supreme and inferior courts is general, and the clause assigning original jurisdiction to the Supreme Court contains no negative or restrictive words," means there is no limit on the authority of the Court to say whatever it wants about the law.

When a majority of conservatives sit on the Supreme Court, the law promotes corporate interests.

When a majority of socialists sit on the Supreme Court, the law promotes social welfare justice.

Marshall's entire bogus judicial edifice of judicial review rests on the synthetic, imaginary concept that "We the People" created the Constitution.

A truthful and honest description of history would state that "We the People" is really 37 elites, who masqueraded as "We the People."

In McCulloch v. Maryland, (1819), Chief Justice Marshall wrote a unanimous opinion that the laws adopted by the federal government are the unquestioned supreme law of the land, over any conflicting laws adopted by state governments.

In a re-play of the arguments over the text of the 10th Amendment involving power "expressly" delegated from the states to the Federal government, Marshall turned the 10th Amendment on its head by ruling that the Constitution granted to the Federal government unstated, unwritten, "implied" powers over the states.

If Madison had not intervened against inserting the word "expressly" into the 10th amendment, Marshall's justification for adopting "implied" powers would have been evaded. In the first place, Marshall argues that it was not the states that delegated powers, it was "We the People."

In the second place, he argues that since the states did not preclude "implied" powers in the 10th Amendment, that implied powers must therefore be authorized.

The State of Maryland argued that,

> The powers of the General Government, it has been said, are delegated by the States, who alone are truly sovereign, and must be exercised in subordination to the States, who alone possess supreme dominion.

Marshall argued that "We the People," granted the authority to the Federal government, not the states, and that after "We the People" granted this supreme power, the citizens had no more power to give.

Marshall wrote,

> Those powers are not given by the people of a single State. They are given by the people of the United States, to a Government whose laws, made in pursuance of the Constitution, are declared to be

supreme. Consequently, the people of a single State cannot confer a sovereignty which will extend over them... the Constitution derives its whole authority. The government proceeds directly from the people; is "ordained and established" in the name of the people, and is declared to be ordained, The assent of the States in their sovereign capacity is implied in calling a convention, and thus submitting that instrument to the people. But the people were at perfect liberty to accept or reject it, and their act was final...It has been said that the people had already surrendered all their powers to the State sovereignties, and had nothing more to give.

Marshall cited the penumbra of implied powers that he saw Article I, Section 8, the "Necessary and Proper Clause," which gave Congress the power to establish a national bank.

Not only did Marshall envision a penumbra that allowed the Federal Government to create a Bank, his penumbra also implied that the U. S. Government could own 20% of the stock of the bank, along with 4000 private, wealthy investors.

Marshall wrote,

> Among the enumerated powers, we do not find that of establishing a bank or creating a corporation. But there is no phrase in the instrument which, like the Articles of Confederation, excludes incidental or implied powers and which requires that everything granted shall be expressly and minutely described. Even the 10th Amendment, which was framed for the purpose of quieting the excessive jealousies which had been excited, omits the word "expressly," and declares only that the powers "not delegated to the United States, nor prohibited to the States, are reserved to the States or to the people," thus leaving the question whether the particular power which may become the subject of

contest has been delegated to the one Government, or prohibited to the other.

Consequently, the implied powers, not cited in the Constitution, but not "expressly prohibited," in Article 10, granted the government the authority to charter a bank, and to own stock in the bank, with other private and foreign investors.

Marshall wrote,

> The bill for incorporating the Bank of the United States did not steal upon an unsuspecting legislature and pass unobserved. Its principle was completely understood, and was opposed with equal zeal and ability. After being resisted first in the fair and open field of debate, and afterwards in the executive cabinet, with as much persevering talent as any measure has ever experienced, and being supported by arguments which convinced minds as pure and as intelligent as this country can boast, it became a law…it is the unanimous and decided opinion of this Court that the act to incorporate the Bank of the United States is a law made in pursuance of the Constitution, and is a part of the supreme law of the land.

In a comprehensive, chilling statement of Federalist totalitarian ideology, Marshall argued that political power must be taken away from the states, in order to be exercised exclusively by the Supreme Court.

His description of the totalitarian powers of the Federal government is a mirror image of Hobbes' Leviathan that compelled obedience to the rule of law.

The logic of subverting the Articles with Madison's constitution, was described by Marshall.

Marshall wrote,

> it was deemed necessary to change this alliance into an effective Government, possessing great and sovereign powers and acting directly on the people, the necessity of referring it to the people, and of deriving its powers directly from them, was felt and acknowledged by all.

Only the Federal elites could hold power, but their totalitarian paternalism would exercise the power for the benefit of common citizens.

Marshall wrote,

> Its powers are granted by them, ("We the People") and are to be exercised directly on them, and for their benefit.

Marshall's Leviathan had awesome, unlimited powers, and just like in Hobbes, once the citizens granted the elites power, there was no recourse.

Marshall wrote,

> It is the Government of all; its powers are delegated by all; it represents all, and acts for all. Though any one State may be willing to control its operations, no State is willing to allow others to control them. The nation, on those subjects on which it can act, must necessarily bind its component parts. But this question is not left to mere reason; the people have, in express terms, decided it by saying, "this Constitution, and the laws of the United States, which shall be made in pursuance thereof," "shall be the supreme law of the land," and by requiring that the members of the State legislatures and the officers of the executive and judicial departments of the States shall take the oath of fidelity to it.

The consequence of Marshall's "implied" power is not seen from the perspective of legal jurisprudence. The consequence is the exercise of raw political power to use the resources of government to benefit one social class over another social class.

By 1819, the Second Bank was the largest, most profitable, financial institution in the world, and its investors included 1000 wealthy European investors, which is the precursor event in the establishment of the global financial deep state ties between U. S. banks, and foreign banks.

As is the historical case of all asset speculation and money inflation caused by the financial elites, the Second Bank failed to control money growth, leading to an asset-based financial collapse in 1819.

Then, following the well-known fiscal policy of the elites, the Bank used a tight money policy to inflict financial damage on common citizens in the form of high unemployment and collapsing real estate farm values.

As a special bonus for the elites, as a result of the fiscal policies of the Bank, the directors of the Baltimore Branch of the Bank were able to buy up the farmer's land, for pennies on the dollar, when he farmers could not repay their mortgages in the required gold and silver.

Continuing the charade of "We the People," in Barron v. Mayor of Baltimore, (1833), the Supreme Court ruled that:

> The constitution was ordained and established by the people of the United States for themselves, for their own government, and not for the government of the individual states. . . . The people of the United States framed such a government for the United States as they supposed best adapted to their situation and best calculated to promote their interests.

In League v. De Young, (1837), the Supreme Court ruled that "The Constitution of the United States was made by, and for the protection of, the people of the United States."

In White v. Hart, (1872), the Supreme Court extended the charade by stating:

The National Constitution was, as its preamble recites, ordained and established by the people of the United States. It created not a confederacy of States, but a government of individuals."

The decision in White v. Hart was based upon the precedent of Martin v. Hunter's Lessee, (1816), where the Court ruled:

> The constitution of the United States was ordained and established, not by the states in their sovereign capacities, but . . . , as the preamble of the constitution declares, by 'the people of the United States.' . . . The constitution was not, therefore, necessarily carved out of existing state sovereignties, nor a surrender of powers already existing in state institutions . . .

In Yick Wo v. Hopkins, (1886), the Court ruled:

> Sovereignty itself is, of course, not subject to law, for it is the author and source of law; but in our system, while sovereign powers are delegated to the agencies of government, sovereignty itself remains with the people, by whom and for whom all government exists and acts.

In Chae Chan Ping v. United States, (1889), the Supreme Court unanimously ruled,

> While each state was originally recognized as sovereign unto itself, the Supreme Court held that the "United States of America" consists of only one sovereign nation with respect to foreign affairs and

international relations; the individual states may not conduct foreign relations.

When the Supreme Court finds that it is politically convenient to re-establish the fantasy that the states, not "We the People," created the Constitution, it reverts to the language of "federalism."

In re Debs, (1895), the Supreme Court reasserted the powers of Leviathan to compel obedience, by arguing that:

> While, under the dual system which prevails with us, the powers of government are distributed between the State and the Nation, and while the latter is properly styled a government of enumerated powers, yet within the limits of such enumeration, it has all the attributes of sovereignty, and, in the exercise of those enumerated powers, acts directly upon the citizen, and not through the intermediate agency of the State. The entire strength of the nation may be used to enforce in any part of the land the full and free exercise of all national powers and the security of all rights entrusted by the Constitution to its care. The strong arm of the national government may be put forth to brush away all obstructions to the freedom of interstate commerce or the transportation of the mails. If the emergency arises, the army of the Nation, and all its militia, are at the service of the Nation to compel obedience to its laws.

In Jacobson v. Massachusetts (1905), the Supreme Court continued its assault on state sovereignty, using "We the People," as the bludgeon:

> The very opening words of the Constitution mark a radical departure: "We the People of the United States." That language was at striking variance with the norm, for in earlier documents, including the 1778 treaty of alliance with France, the Articles of Confederation, and the 1783 Treaty of Paris

recognizing American independence, the word "People" was not used, and the phrase "the United States" was followed immediately by a listing of the states ("viz., New Hampshire, Massachusetts Bay, Rhode Island and Providence Plantations," and so on down to Georgia).

The only purpose served by the text "We the People," is to empower the Federal government over state governments.

In United States v. Boyer, (1898), the Court ruled:

> The preamble never can be resorted to, to enlarge the powers confided to the general government, or any of its departments. It cannot confer any power per se. It can never amount, by implication, to an enlargement of any power expressly given. It can never be the legitimate source of any implied power, when otherwise withdrawn from the constitution. Its true office is to expound the nature and extent and application of the powers actually conferred by the constitution, and not substantively to create them.

The charade of "We the People," as the law givers continues in Carter v. Carter Coal Co., (1936):

> The Constitution itself is in every real sense a law— the lawmakers being the people themselves, in whom under our system all political power and sovereignty primarily resides, and through whom such power and sovereignty primarily speaks. It is by that law, and not otherwise, that the legislative, executive, and judicial agencies which it created exercise such political authority as they have been permitted to possess. The Constitution speaks for itself in terms so plain that to misunderstand their import is not rationally possible. 'We the People of the United States,' it says, 'do ordain and establish this Constitution.' Ordain and establish! These are definite words of enactment, and

without more would stamp what follows with the dignity and character of law.

All of which is very logical and legally defensible, except for the fact that "We the People," did not ordain and establish the Constitution.

"We the People," does not exist.

The Constitution was established and ordained by a self-selected group of 37 elites.

In 1930, Justice Oliver Wendell Holmes, Jr., in one of his dissents, re-stated George Mason's objections to Madison' Constitution.

Holmes wrote:

> I have not yet adequately expressed the more than anxiety that I feel at the ever increasing scope given to the Fourteenth Amendment in cutting down what I believe to be the constitutional rights of the States. As the decisions now stand, I see hardly any limit but the sky to the invalidating of those rights if they happen to strike a majority of this Court as for any reason undesirable. I cannot believe that the Amendment was intended to give us carte blanche to embody our economic or moral beliefs in its prohibitions. Yet I can think of no narrower reason that seems to me to justify the present and the earlier decisions to which I have referred. Of course the words due process of law, if taken in their literal meaning, have no application to this case; and while it is too late to deny that they have been given a much more extended and artificial signification, still we ought to remember the great caution shown by the Constitution in limiting the power of the States, and should be slow to construe the clause in the Fourteenth Amendment as committing to the Court, with no guide but the Court's own

> discretion, the validity of whatever laws the States may pass.

In United States v. Butler, (1936), the Court flip-flopped back to the principle of delegated state power in order to empower one of Roosevelt's schemes that denied a farmer the right to grow wheat on his land for his own use.

> From the accepted doctrine that the United States is a government of delegated powers, it follows that those not expressly granted, or reasonably to be implied from such as are conferred, are reserved to the states or to the people. To forestall any suggestion to the contrary, the Tenth Amendment was adopted. The same proposition, otherwise stated, is that powers not granted are prohibited. None to regulate agricultural production is given, and therefore legislation by Congress for that purpose is forbidden.

The dirty little secret of "We the People," is that there was absolutely nothing wrong with the Articles of Confederation that could not have been fixed by some easy, simple modifications.

As the natural rights populist Philanthropos argued, in 1787, that there was nothing seriously wrong with the Articles of Incorporation that Madison could not have easily fixed at the convention in Philadelphia.

Philanthropos wrote,

> Our present constitution, (the Articles), with a few additional powers to Congress, seems better calculated to preserve the rights and defend the liberties of our citizens, than the one proposed, (by Madison), without proper amendments. Let us therefore, for once, show our judgment and solidity by continuing it, (the Articles), and prove the opinion to be erroneous, that

levity and fickleness are not only the foibles of our tempers, but the reigning principles in these states.

But fixing the Articles was not the intent of Madison.

Madison intended to subjugate the states to a consolidated central government, and for that purpose Madison had to make believe that the states did not create the new government.

Madison came up with an ingenious deception that a mythical entity, "We the People," created the new government.

Madison left it up to his Federalist friends on the Supreme Court to do the dirty work of eviscerating the sovereignty of state governments.

Allegiance to the rule of law, noted Hamilton, depended upon a unique set of cultural values, to which citizens voluntarily adhere.

Madison's institutional separation of powers and the "Supremacy Clause," that eviscerated the states, were only the mechanisms of power.

Unlike the Articles of Confederation, Madison deliberately failed to provide the required set of common cultural values, which would bind citizens to voluntary allegiance to the rule of law.

Today, Madison's defect has allowed the country to be ideologically split between socialists, who want more socialism, and natural rights conservatives, who want more individual liberty.

Madison's defect cannot be fixed because the document did not state the common cultural values that were contained in the Declaration.

"We the People," and "Form a More Perfect Union," are not a substitute for "life, liberty, and the pursuit of happiness."

There is nothing, today, that binds citizens into a common nation with a common mission.

Madison knew exactly what he was doing, and he used great deception and guile to overthrow the Articles and subordinate the states to his central government.

Madison wrote in Federalist #45,

> The powers delegated by the proposed Constitution to the federal government, are few and defined. Those which are to remain in the State governments are numerous and indefinite.

Madison continued,

> The powers reserved to the several States will extend to all the objects which, in the ordinary course of affairs, concern the lives, liberties, and properties of the people, and the internal order, improvement, and prosperity of the State.

Madison knew at the time he promised that the powers of the central government would be limited, was a lie. His statement was propaganda to allay fears of the citizens about centralized power.

He knew that his logic of consolidation was based upon the idea that "We the People," delegated power, which is why he argued, during the convention, that there was no need for a Bill of Rights.

During the Convention, the delegates were mostly set against the inclusion of a bill of rights in the new Constitution, defeating efforts by George Mason and Elbridge Gerry to consider one.

Madison played both sides of the issue, saying in a letter to Thomas Jefferson,

> I have always been in favor of a bill of rights... At the same time I have never thought the omission a material defect, nor been anxious to supply it even by subsequent amendment.

Five of the states that conditionally ratified the Constitution included a list of amendments that would be required in the new Constitution, if they were to extend unconditional approval.

After Madison first fought against the inclusion of a Bill of Rights, he switched sides. In his election campaign against James Monroe for the new U.S. House, vowed to fight for a bill of rights.

He informed the Congress on May 4, 1789, that he intended to introduce the topic formally on May 25; but on May 4, the Congress was embroiled in a lengthy debate on import duties, and when May 25 rolled around, the debate continued.

He rose again on June 8 to introduce the subject, but he was blocked, with other members noting that the Congress had more pressing matters to attend to.

In the ensuing debate in Congress, about the 10th Amendment, Madison modified the text to take out the word "expressly" because of the legal damage the word would do to the centralized power of the government.

Madison argued that the Articles of Confederation had been created by the 13 states, while this new constitution was created by "We the People."

Madison wrote,

> Should all the states adopt it, it will be then a government established by the thirteen states of

> America, not through the intervention of the legislatures, but by the people at large. In this particular respect the distinction between the existing and the proposed governments is very material. The existing system (The Articles), has been derived from the dependent derivative authority of the legislatures of the states; whereas, this is derived from the superior power of the people.

Madison cited North Carolina's opposition to the Constitution as his motive for including the Bill of Rights.

Madison wrote:

> I allude in a particular manner to those two States that have not thought fit to throw themselves into the bosom of the Confederacy. It is a desirable thing, on our part as well as theirs, that a re-union should take place as soon as possible. I have no doubt, if we proceed to take those steps which would be prudent and requisite at this juncture, that in a short time we should see that disposition prevailing in those States which have not come in, that we have seen prevailing in those States which have embraced the constitution.

Madison then invoked his deception that the Bill of Rights could be adopted without damaging the supreme power of the central government.

His deception hinged on excluding the word "expressly" in the 10th Amendment.

Madison wrote,

> I do conceive that the constitution may be amended; that is to say, if all power is subject to abuse, that then it is possible the abuse of the powers of the General Government may be guarded against in a more secure manner than is now done, while no one advantage

> arising from the exercise of that power shall be damaged or endangered by it…(the amendments can be adopted) without endangering any part of the constitution, which is considered as essential to the existence of the Government by those who promoted its adoption.

Madison's opening argument for the amendments cites the authority of "We the People," who granted the new government its powers. Madison placed the text for "We the People" in the Preamble.

Madison wrote,

> First, That there be prefixed to the constitution, (in the Preamble) a declaration, that all power is originally rested in, and consequently derived from, the people… The powers not delegated by this constitution, nor prohibited by it to the States, are reserved to the States respectively.

Madison then switches sides to argue that specific powers not delegated by either the states or "the people," are discretionary powers of the government.

The Bill of Rights could be added, argued Madison, because those rights did not interfere with the discretionary power of the government.

Madison wrote,

> It (the central government) has certain discretionary powers with respect to the means, which may admit of abuse to a certain extent, in the same manner as the powers of the State Governments under their constitutions may to an indefinite extent; because in the constitution of the United States, there is a clause granting to Congress the power to make all laws which shall be necessary and proper for carrying into execution all the powers vested in the Government of

the United States, or in any department or officer thereof; this enables them to fulfil every purpose for which the Government was established.

In other words, the inclusion of the Bill of Rights was not significant for Madison as long as the new government was not bound by the word "expressly," in the 10th Amendment.

And, as long as the Necessary and Proper clause remained untouched, Madison had succeeded in creating a central government of unlimited power over the states.

Patrick Henry got the analysis of Madison's scheme of "We the People," exactly right in his arguments against Virginia's adoption of the Constitution.

Henry wrote,

> I have the highest veneration for those gentlemen; but sir, give me leave to demand, What right had they to say, We, the people? My political curiosity, exclusive of my anxious solicitude for the public welfare, leads me to ask: Who authorized them to speak the language of, We, the people, instead of, We, the states? States are the characteristics and the soul of confederation. If the states be not the agents of this compact, it must be one, great, consolidated, national government, of the people of all states.

Madison's constitution was "one, great, consolidated national government," as identified by Patrick Henry.

In just 6 short years, "We the People," Federalists deployed a set of tyrannical acts, designed to eliminate their natural rights opponents. Jefferson was so alarmed at the tyranny that he wrote the Kentucky Resolutions to set the record straight that the states had delegated power to the Constitution, not "We the People."

Madison switched sides and joined Jefferson in promoting the Kentucky Resolutions, as if he had never promoted "We the People."

Jefferson wrote,

> Resolved, that the several States composing the United States of America, are not united on the principle of unlimited submission to their general government; but that by compact under the style and title of a Constitution for the United States and of amendments thereto, they constituted a general government for special purposes, delegated to that government certain definite powers, reserving each State to itself, the residuary mass of right to their own self-government; and that whensoever the general government assumes undelegated powers, its acts are unauthoritative, void, and of no force: That to this compact each State acceded as a State, and is an integral party, its co-States forming, as to itself, the other party....each party has an equal right to judge for itself, as well of infractions as of the mode and measure of redress.

As was the case of the unresolved issue of slavery in Madison's Constitution, the issue of "We the People," was never resolved, both issues leading to the slaughter of 750,000 citizens in the Civil War.

Jefferson's Kentucky Resolution was not successful in re-establishing the sovereignty of states.

Just prior to the start of the Civil War, Jefferson Davis tried again to reassert the sovereignty of states in his resolution of 1860, in Congress.

Davis wrote,

> Resolved, That the union of these States rests on the equality of rights and privileges among its members, and that it is especially the duty of the Senate, which

represents the States in their sovereign capacity, to resist all attempts to discriminate either in relation to person or property, so as, in the Territories—which are the common possession of the United States—to give advantages to the citizens of one State which are not equally secured to those of every other State.

The issue, still today, has never been resolved, leading 38 states, in 2010, to introduce resolutions in their state legislatures to reassert the principle of state sovereignty.

The unresolved issue has led to a fundamental, irresolvable conflict between socialists and natural rights conservatives over the future of the nation.

The socialists, just like the earlier Federalists, want an all-powerful centralized government to impose their ideology of social welfare justice on all citizens.

The socialists point to the text "We the People," as their justification for the legality of imposing their ideology. Like the charade of the 37 elites who wrote the Constitution, the socialists today claim that they are "We the People."

The socialists are correct in their interpretation of "We the People." Madison deliberately failed to include the set of common cultural values that would serve to bind citizens in a common national endeavor.

The national mission could just as easily be the imposition of socialism as the imposition of freedom.

The cultural values of individual freedom are not compatible with the cultural values of socialism, and the two cultures cannot peacefully co-exist within a sovereign national boundary.

The peaceful resolution of the intractable problem of socialism in America is to partition the nation into free and slave states, and to allow socialists to emigrate to the slave states.

The free states of the Democratic Republic of America would ratify a new constitution that would restore the priority of states over the national government, and extinguish Madison's fraud of "We the People," forever.

The restoration of state sovereignty in the Democratic Republic of America is accomplished with the following text of the new Constitituion:

Preamble:

We, the citizens of the Democratic Republic of America, establish this constitutional contract between our respective states and the National Government of the Democratic Republic of America.

We solemnly swear and affirm that we establish this contract to preserve and protect the natural and civil rights of citizens in each state, and to protect and defend the sovereignty of each state and the nation, from foreign and domestic threats.

Principles of Government:

5. "...that the National Government is instituted to allow individual citizens to pursue individual happiness and to limit the arbitrary application of government power over the lives of individuals..."

6. "...that individual citizens who freely give their consent to form a government through constitutional conventions are bound by the original contract until the operation of the government becomes destructive to the original intent of obtaining individual freedom and the pursuit of happiness..."

7. "...that the citizens of each state have mechanisms in place in the constitutional contract to modify or abolish the

governments that have been created that have become destructive to the ideals and goals under which the National Government is instituted, including the right to vote on remaining a member of the national government in a referendum to be held every 20 years from the date of admittance..."

8. "...that the parties to the constitutional contract are individual citizens acting through their elected representatives at the state and national levels of government..."

9. "...that the National Government is created by this union of states and the National Government shall never usurp the sovereign power or authority of the individual states or the sovereignty of the citizens in each state and that states have an inalienable right to call a convention of the states, without Congressional approval, to modify, amend, or abolish this Constitutional Contract."
Clauses of Constitutional Articles:

That all citizens in the respective states have a natural right to own and use weapons, and that the National Government shall make no laws which abridge the right of law-abiding citizens from owning, keeping and bearing weapons.

That citizens have a civil right of action against elected representatives or agents of the National Government, for violation of these natural rights, upon a presentation of a motion of grievance to a Grand Jury of 18 citizens, who shall hear the case and determine the outcome and set the penalties for the violation by a majority vote.

The a citizens Grand Jury in any State retains the right of initiating a citizen initiative on legislative proposals by a petition to the House of Representatives, which must respond to the petition within 30 days of receipt.

The House of Representatives shall represent the interests and rights of citizens in each state.

The Senate of the Democratic Republic of America shall be composed of one Senator elected from each state.

The Senators represent the collective corporate interests of the state.

The National Congress shall have the power to issue government bonds, and to borrow money on the credit of the Democratic Republic of America. All proposals to borrow money or issue debt shall occur once in the two year budget cycle, and all proposals to issue debt must be approved by 50% of the State legislatures of the Democratic Republic of America, no later than January 21 of the year of issuance.

The judicial power of the District and Supreme Court extends to cases arising under the Constitution of the Democratic Republic of America.

A decision by the Supreme Court becomes the supreme law of the land for issues pertaining exclusively to the Constitution of the Democratic Republic of America.

This Constitution, and the laws made by the National Congress, or which shall be made, under the Authority of the Democratic Republic, shall be the supreme Law of the Land for laws and cases exclusively pertaining to the National Government.

Full Faith and Credit shall be given in each state to the public acts, records, and judicial proceedings of every other state. And the Senate of the National Congress may by general laws prescribe the manner in which such acts, records and proceedings shall be proved, and the effect thereof.

Upon a petition for admission from a state legislature, new states may be admitted by the Senate into this Union.

Conclusion.

When Thomas Burke wrote the Articles, he proposed that all sovereign power was in the states separately and that the federal government held enumerated powers.

He wrote that each state,

> retains its sovereignty, freedom and independence…and any right which is not by this confederation expressly delegated to the United States in Congress assembled.

This text, by Burke, has caused 230 years of confusion about state's rights because citizens assume that the states delegated powers to the federal government.

The reason that 38 states are passing resolutions about state's rights today is that those legislatures want to restore the original contract between the states and the central government.

When Madison overthrew the Articles with "We the People," he did not allow a head-to-head vote between the Articles and his constitution.

The only question about ratification was a yes-or-no on the "We the People," constitution, in a charade of "citizen" conventions.

Ensuing generations of citizens did not realize that Madison had disconnected his constitution from Jefferson's Declaration, and connected it to the British social class mixed government model, but without the British safeguards against tyranny.

The citizens did not figure out that Madison disconnected his constitution from the Articles, either.

Natural rights conservatives are confronting a constitutional crisis because the socialists despise the founding principles of this nation.

There is nothing in Madison's constitution that prohibits the socialists from implementing their "fundamental transformation" of America, because their interpretation of America as a racist, evil state is as valid as the natural rights conservative interpretation of American principles.

The best solution for restoration of states rights is to start over at the point of the Articles, and create a new constitution for the Democratic Republic of America that re-establishes the national government as a contract between the states and the delegated powers the states grant to the central government.

Chapter 6.

The President's Responsibilities in Defending National Sovereignty and the Natural Rights of Individuals.

Many academic historians have expressed surprise that Madison failed to describe the mission of the president in his Virginia Plan, of 1787.

His plan had only two provisions that addressed the topic of the Office of the President.

Madison had explained to George Washington, one month before the Constitutional Convention, that he had not been able to come up with the duties and mission of the president.

Madison wrote,

> I have scarcely ventured as yet to form my own opinion either of the manner in which the executive) ought to be constituted or of the authorities with which it ought to be cloathed.

The explanation for Madison's uncertainty about the president's role is that his British social class mixed government model did not have a president.

The British system has a prime minister, appointed by the King.

Part of Madison's intent in overthrowing the Articles of Confederation was that it did not contain a chief executive that functioned like the British prime minister, who administered the prerogatives of the King.

Madison was not interested in a federal confederation of states, he wanted a unified centralized national government that was lead by an authority figure.

In Great Britain, the prime minister is accountable to the King, and Madison was not certain how the American President would function, in the absence of a King.

Madison relied on his earlier experience in writing the Virginia Constitution to write the new U. S. Constitution 11 years later.

When Madison wrote the Virginia Constitution, in 1776, he replicated parts of the British model, including the role of the King's Privy Council, redefined as the Virginia Council of State.

In Virginia's model, the role of the prime minister in reporting to the King in Britain was replaced by Virginia's plantation elite, who were appointed to serve as the new Privy Council.

In other words, in the Virginia model of government, the plantation elite were equivalent to the British nobility.

Throughout the Constitutional Convention, Madison never gave up on the idea that some form of Privy Council should act in the capacity of giving advice to the Office of the President.

Madison's role model of President was Lord North who was Prime Minister of Great Britain from January, 1770 to March, 1782.

In December of 1766, the King appointed North to the Privy Council and by early 1767, he was called to attend Cabinet meetings.

When Charles Townshend died in, September of 1767, the King appointed Lord North the Chancellor of the Exchequer.

On January 31, 1770, King George appointed Lord North prime minister.

The Prime Minister of the United Kingdom is the head of the United Kingdom government. The Prime Minister and Cabinet are collectively accountable for their policies and actions to the Monarch.

The office of prime minister is not established by any statute or constitutional document but exists only by long-established convention, which stipulates that the monarch must appoint as Prime Minister the person most likely to command the confidence of the House of Commons.

The absence of a written British constitution compounded Madison's uncertainty about the role and function of the President.

The relationships between the Prime Minister and the Sovereign, Parliament and Cabinet are defined largely by these unwritten conventions of the constitution.

Many of the Prime Minister's executive and legislative powers are actually royal prerogatives which are still formally vested in the Sovereign, who remains the head of state.

One of the reasons that Madison initially supported calling George Washington a King is because an American King would more nearly operate like the British King.

One of the reasons Hamilton supported appointing the President for life was that a life-time appointment would more nearly replicate the British monarchy.

In the British system, the Parliament, beginning around 1687, effectively dispersed the powers of the Crown, entrusting its authority to responsible ministers who served on a newer version of the King's Privy Council.

Prior to the start of the Revolution, the King's Privy Council had the King's authority to impose laws and veto laws in the American colonies.

Prior to the start of the Revolution, Virginia's Council consisted of 12 of Virginia's richest planters, who were appointed by the King's Privy Council.

The King's appointments to the Council were life-time appointments.

The Governor's Council in Virginia gave advice to the Royal Governor in Virginia, on behalf of the King.

The Governor's Council in Virginia served as justices in the Virginia judicial system.

The members of the Council held a dual position of power by serving in the legislature of Virginia. The members of the Council served as the Senate of Virginia, just like the House of Lords in England.

In other words, the Council was a combination of the executive, the Court, and the legislature in Virginia.

It was from was this combination of power that Madison realized that Virginia's aristocracy had derived privilege and power from the British royalty, in the form of the King's Council.

In Madison's mind, combining the power of the Council with the President would form a "more perfect union."

The "more perfect union," was not a union of states because "We, the People," created the constitution. The more perfect union was a union of executive power with the power of the natural aristocracy to have unchallenged authority.

The power of the British House of Commons in checking the authority of the Council was a model for Madison in his system of checks and balances.

As the British system evolved, the prime minister was also the Head of the British Treasury, and this dual position of power was attractive to Madison because the Prime Minister would have the power to compel the payment of government debt in gold and silver.

One of the reasons that Madison failed to address the role of political parties in his political model was that the British system depended on all political parties being loyal to the King. In Britain, there was only one political party, the King's Party, and in Madison's conception, the natural aristocracy would replicate the King's Party.

In the American setting, the King's Party would be the 37 Federalists who signed the Constitution. Madison did not address the issue of political parties because he assumed that America would have only one dominant party, called the Federalists.

In replicating the British system when he wrote the Virginia Constitution in 1776, Madison eliminated the right to vote for common citizens. Only the natural aristocracy possessed the exclusive power to vote in his constitution, a feature of politics that lasted in Virginia until 1820.

Madison stated in Federalist # 40 that the constitutional convention of 1787 created a mixed government.

In Madison's conception, the British mixed government was comprised of three parties, the one, the few, and the many.

In the British context, the one was the King, the few were the nobility, and the many were the common citizens

In Madison's American version of mixed government, the one was the President, the few were the natural aristocracy, who served in the Senate, and the many the common citizens, who elected representatives for the House of Representatives.

Madison explained, in Federalist #47, how his rendition of mixed government would operate. Madison wrote,

In the very Constitution to which it is prefixed, a partial mixture of powers has been admitted. The executive magistrate has a qualified negative on the legislative body, and the Senate, which is a part of the legislature, is a court of impeachment for members both of the executive and judiciary departments. The members of the judiciary department, again, are appointable by the executive department, and removable by the same authority on the address of the two legislative branches.

While Madison cited Montesquieu as his primary source of authority for his ideas on mixed government, he also cited the Greek philosopher Polybius.

Madison referred to Polybius in Federalist #63.

Polybius outlined three simple forms of constitution each categorized according to the number of its ruling body:

- monarchy (rule by the one),
- aristocracy (rule by the few), and
- democracy (rule by the many).

In the Polybius theory, a type of historical determinism cycles each form of government through predictable phases.

Each form of government degenerates, over time, into three forms of predictable corruption. The monarchy degenerates into tyranny, the aristocracy degenerates into corrupt oligarchy, and democracy ends up in mob-rule.

In his theory, Polybius explained that each form of government was replaced by the next form, in a continuous cycle that repeated itself.

It was this historical dynamic that Madison used as his logic in forming the constitution, and formed the basis of the powers of the Office of the President.

Madison's first resolution about the President in his Virginia Plan stated:

> Resolved. that a national Executive be instituted to consist of a single person. to be chosen by the National Legislature. for the term of seven years. with power to carry into execution the national Laws, to appoint to Offices in cases not otherwise provided for to be ineligible a second time, and to be removable on impeachment and conviction of mal practice or neglect of duty. to receive a fixed stipend, by which he may be compensated for the devotion of his time to public service to be paid out of the national Treasury.

Madison defined the civil rules of procedure of electing the President, without describing the mission of the President. His main idea was that the President should have a shared veto power with the Council of Revision, composed of the executive and members of the federal judiciary.

As he argued during the Convention, his form of government called for a type of passive, administrator executive that shared power with a Council of State.

At the Convention, Madison stated,

> Instead, therefore, of contenting ourselves with laying down the theory in the Constitution, that each department ought to be separate and distinct, it was proposed to add a defensive power to each, which should maintain the theory in practice. In so doing, we did not blend the departments together. We erected effectual barriers for keeping them separate. The most regular example of this theory was in the British Constitution. Yet it was not only the practice there to admit the Judges to a seat in the Legislature, and in the Executive Councils, and submit to their previous examination all laws of a certain description, but it was a part of their Constitution that the Executive might

negative any law whatever; a part of their Constitution which had been universally regarded as calculated for the preservation of the whole.

The passive administrative President was an essential feature of Madison's government because he anticipated that special interest factions were the only parties to the government.

He deliberately left out how the President would defend the national public purpose in his national government.

Rather, Madison's rules of separation of power were the instruments to balance and check factional political power in order to insure that social elites, (the few), who made important decisions on behalf of all society, were insulated from the democratic tyranny that could be imposed by the majority of people, (the many).

Madison wrote,

> The next relation is, to the sources from which the ordinary powers of government are to be derived. The House of Representatives will derive its powers from the people of America; and the people will be represented in the same proportion, and on the same principle, as they are in the legislature of a particular State. So far the government is NATIONAL, not FEDERAL. The Senate, on the other hand, will derive its powers from the States, as political and coequal societies; and these will be represented on the principle of equality in the Senate.

The two special financial interests that Madison envisioned competing against each other, in a national government, did not require an active President.

Consequently, Madison did not include any language about the mission of the President, other than administering the laws.

Madison's logic in omitting the mission of the President was based in his assumption that the natural aristocracy possessed virtue, and would make beneficial decisions on behalf of all citizens.

In Federalist #37, Madison writes,

> among the great variety of interests, parties, and sects which it embraces, a coalition of a majority of the whole society could seldom take place on any other principles than those of justice and the general good. . .we are to presume that in general they (the few), will be somewhat distinguished also by those qualities which entitle them to it, and which promise a sincere and scrupulous regard to the nature of their engagements.

Madison wrote,

> The accumulation of all powers, legislative, executive and judicial in the same hands, whether of one, a few, or many, and whether hereditary, self-appointed, or elective, may justly be pronounced the very definition of tyranny.

For Madison, the purpose of government is not to provide a mechanism of rights claims and reciprocation of trust among citizens.

Rather, Madison's rules were the instruments to balance and check factional political power in order to insure that social elites, the natural leaders, who made important decisions on behalf of all society, were insulated from the tyranny that could be imposed by the people, through democratic procedures.

As Madison stated, "the chief object of government is to regulate "these various and interfering interests."

As it turned out, 230 years later, the omission of the mission of the Office of President led to a series of rogue Presidents, and ultimately to the centralized elite tyranny, called the swamp.

A constitution that is silent on the mission of the President acts to empower an unstated grant of power for a rogue President to take the law into his own hands.

Following the cycle of mixed government in Polybius, Madison's constitution is an abject failure because the aristocratic phase of his mixed government ended in corrupt tyranny, and Madison never had the confidence in the citizens to allow for democracy.

In other words, Madison's rules had the effect of truncating the next phase of democracy in the mixed government model of Polybius.

The arguments about the power of the President took place within the much bigger context about a national consolidated government versus a federal confederation of states.

When the delegates from the southern states arrived in Philadelphia, and figured out Madison's intent in eradicating the Articles of Confederation, they asked a series of questions about Madison's purpose.

Those questions later influenced the debate about the Office of President.

From Madison's notes taken during the debates,

Mr. PINCKNEY wished to know of Mr. Randolph whether he meant to abolish the state governments altogether. Mr. Randolph replied that he meant by these general propositions merely to introduce the particular ones which explained the outlines of the system he had in view.

Gen. PINCKNEY expressed a doubt whether the act of [the Confederation] Congress recommending the Convention, or the commissions of the deputies to it could authorize a discussion of a system founded on different principles from the federal constitution.

Mr. GERRY seemed to entertain the same doubt.

Mr. DICKINSON The division of the country into distinct States formed the other principal source of stability. This division ought therefore to be maintained, and considerable powers to be left with the States. This was the ground of his consolation for the future fate of his country. Without this, and in case of a consolidation of the States into one great republic, we might read its fate in the history of smaller ones. A limited monarchy he considered as one of the best governments in the world. It was not certain that the same blessings were derivable from any other form. It was certain that equal blessings had never yet been derived from any of the republican forms

Soon after the delegates realized that "We, the People," and not the states, wrote their new constitution, they limited their attention on the Office of the President to two primary issues:

> Should the Office of President be one person, three people, or a mix of the President and a new form of Privy Council, who advised the President.

> Should the Office of President be an equal co-branch, with the same authority as the Congress and Supreme Court, or should the President be more like an administrator of laws passed by Congress.

Solving those two primary issues depended on how the President was selected, or elected, and the extent of leadership authority the President would have over creating the policies of the new nation.

Both of these issues were complicated by the presence of George Washington, the presumptive new president, or the King, as the delegates would decide.

From Madison's notes:

Mr. SHERMAN was against enabling any one man to stop the will of the whole. No man could be found so far above all the rest in wisdom. The ideal executive was nothing more than an institution for carrying the will of the Legislature into effect.

Mr. WILSON preferred a single magistrate, as giving most energy, dispatch, and responsibility to the office.

Mr. GERRY favored the policy of annexing a council to the executive in order to give weight and inspire confidence.

Mr. RANDOLPH strenuously opposed a unity in the executive magistracy. He regarded it as the fetus of monarchy.... He could not see why the great requisites for the executive department—vigor, dispatch, and responsibility—could not be found in three men as well as in one man. The executive ought to be independent. It ought, therefore, in order to support its independence, to consist of more than one.

Mr. GOUVERNEUR MORRIS. Some check being necessary on the Legislature, the question is, in what hands it should be lodged? On one side, it was contended, that the Executive alone ought to exercise it. He did not think that an Executive appointed for six years, and impeachable whilst in office, would be a very effectual check. On the other side, it was urged, that he ought to be reinforced by the Judiciary department

Against this it was objected, that expositors of laws ought to have no hand in making them, and arguments in favor of this had been drawn from England. What weight was due to them might be easily determined by an attention to facts.

The truth was, that the Judges in England had a great share in the legislation. They are consulted in difficult and doubtful cases. They may be, and some of them are, members of the Legislature. They are, or may be, members of the Privy Council; and can there advise the Executive, as they will do with us if the motion succeeds. The influence the English Judges may have, in the latter capacity, in strengthening the Executive check, cannot be ascertained, as the King, by his influence, in a manner dictates the laws

Mr. MADISON. The objection against a union of the Judiciary and Executive branches, in the revision of the laws, had either no foundation, or was not carried far enough. If such a union was an improper mixture of powers, or such a Judiciary check on the laws was inconsistent with the theory of a free constitution, it was equally so to admit the Executive to any participation in the making of laws; and the revisionary plan ought to be discarded altogether.

For most of June and July, the delegates went around and around these same issues, without resolution.

During those two months, the delegates voted more than 60 times just on the method of electing the president.

They could not make progress on the method of elections until they solved the bigger issue of what powers the president would have.

They could not solve the issue of the powers of the president until they solved the issue of whether the president was one person, or a Council.

At the beginning of August, as a way of trying to resolve the issues about the Office of President, Morris and Pinckney drafted a resolution that they hoped would capture the majority sentiment of the delegates.

Mr. GOUVERNEUR MORRIS, seconded by Mr. PINCKNEY, submitted the following propositions which were, in like manner, referred to the Committee of Detail:

"To assist the President in conducting the public affairs, there shall be a Council of State composed of the following officers:

"1. The Chief Justice of the Supreme Court, who shall from time to time recommend such alterations of and additions to the laws of the United States, as may in his opinion be necessary to the due administration of justice; and such as may promote useful learning and inculcate sound morality throughout the Union. He shall be President of the Council, in the absence of the President.

"2. The Secretary of Domestic Affairs, who shall be appointed by the President, and hold his office during pleasure. It shall be his duty to attend to matters of general police, the state of agriculture and manufactures, the opening of roads and navigations, and the facilitating communications through the United States; and he shall from time to time recommend such measures and establishments as may tend to promote those objects.

"3. The Secretary of Commerce and Finance, who shall also be appointed by the President during pleasure. It shall be his duty to superintend all matters relating to the public finances, to prepare and report plans of revenue and for the regulation of expenditures, and also to recommend such things as may, in his judgment, promote the commercial interests of the United States.

"4. The Secretary of Foreign Affairs, who shall also be appointed by the President during pleasure. It shall be his duty to correspond with all foreign ministers, prepare plans of treaties, and consider such as may be transmitted from abroad; and generally to attend to the interests of the United States in their connexions with foreign powers.

"5. The Secretary of War, who shall also be appointed by the President during pleasure. It shall be his duty to superintend every thing relating to the War department, such as the raising and equipping of troops, the care of military stores, public fortifications, arsenals, and the like; also in time of war to prepare and recommend plans of offence and defence.

"6. The Secretary of the Marine, who shall also be appointed during pleasure. It shall be his duty to superintend every thing relating to the Marine department, the public ships, dock-yards, naval stores, and arsenals; also in the time of war to prepare and recommend plans of offence and defence.

"7. The President shall also appoint a Secretary of State, to hold his office during pleasure; who shall be Secretary to the Council of State, and also public Secretary to the President. It shall be his duty to prepare all public despatches from the President, which he shall countersign. The President may from time to time submit any matter to the discussion of the Council of State, and he may require the written opinions of any one or more of the members. But he shall in all cases exercise his own judgment, and either conform to such opinions, or not, as he may think proper; and every officer above mentioned shall be responsible for his opinion, on the affairs relating to his particular department.

"8. Each of the officers above mentioned shall be liable to impeachment and removal from office, for neglect of duty, malversation, or corruption."

The Committee of Detail was given its task on July 24. The resolution stayed bottled up in the Committee of Detail until the end of August. The job of the Committee of Detail was to add the final details to the resolution, before the adjournment of the Convention, tentatively set for September 13.

The Committee of Detail decided that the title for the president should not be "king." The other issues regarding the mission of the president and the rules for electing the president were left unsolved, to the very last minute.

As he did in failing to address the issue of the morality of slavery, but adding rules and procedures for counting slaves, Madison also failed to explain the mission and purpose of the Office of President. The convention delegates spent their final days in Philadelphia arguing about how the President should be elected and the power of the President, but not addressing the bigger issue of the mission of the President to protect the natural rights of citizens.

The debate in the final 11 days of the Convention empowered the Office without describing what acted as a barrier to a rogue President taking the law into his own hands.

Both proponents and opponents to the Constitution understood the danger of corruption and cabal of a rogue President.

The opponents to Madison's Virginia plan very clearly argued that the Office of President that Madison was creating was an unchecked power that would end in the tyranny of a rogue president. Most of the authority for selecting the President was vested in the unelected Senate.

The Senate was comprised of a very tiny minority of America's natural aristocracy, and Madison's plan empowered the Senate make decisions about the election of the President.

The language the opponents used to describe the tyranny was "creating an aristocracy."

From Madison's notes:

September 4.

Mr. GOVr. MORRIS said,

As the Electors would vote at the same time throughout the U. S. and at so great a distance from

each other, the great evil of cabal was avoided. It would be impossible also to corrupt them. A conclusive reason for making the Senate instead of the Supreme Court the Judge of impeachment, was that the latter was to try the President after the trial of the impeachment.

Mr. PINKNEY stated as objections to the mode of election.

it threw the whole appointment in fact into the hands of the Senate. 2. The Electors will be strangers to the several candidates and of course unable to decide on their comparative merits. 3. It makes the Executive reeligible which will endanger the public liberty. 4. It makes the same body of men which will in fact elect the President his Judges in case of an impeachment.

September 5.

Mr. RUTLIDGE was much opposed to the plan reported by the Committee.

It would throw the whole power into the Senate. He was also against are-eligibility. He moved to postpone the Report under consideration & take up the original plan of appointment by the Legislature, to wit. "He shall be elected by joint ballot by the Legislature to which election a majority of the votes of the members present shall be required: He shall hold his office during the term of seven years; but shall not be elected a second time."

Col. MASON admitted that there were objections to an appointment by the Legislature as originally planned.

He had not yet made up his mind, but would state his objections to the mode proposed by the Committee.

It puts the appointment in fact into the hands of the Senate, as it will rarely happen that a majority of the whole votes will fall on anyone candidate: and as the Existing President will always be one of the 5 highest, his reappointment will of course depend on the Senate. 2. Considering the powers of the President & those of the Senate, if a coalition should be established between these two branches, they will be able to subvert the Constitution—The great objection with him would be removed by depriving the Senate of the eventual election. He accordingly moved to strike out the words "if such number be a majority of that of the electors.

Mr. RANDOLPH. We have in some revolutions of this plan made a bold stroke for Monarchy.

We are now doing the same for an aristocracy. He dwelt on the tendency of such an influence in the Senate over the election of the President in addition to its other powers, to convert that body into a real & dangerous Aristocracy.

Col: MASON. As the mode of appointment is now regulated, he could not forbear expressing his opinion that it is utterly inadmissible.

He would prefer the Government of Prussia to one which will put all power into the hands of seven or eight men, and fix an Aristocracy worse than absolute monarchy. The words "and of their giving their votes" being inserted on motion for that purpose, after the words "The Legislature may determine the time of chusing and assembling the electors."

September 6.

Mr. WILSON said that he had weighed carefully the report of the Committee for remodelling the constitution of the Executive; and on combining it with other parts of the plan, he was obliged to consider the whole as having a dangerous tendency to aristocracy; as throwing a dangerous power into the hands of the Senate. They will have in fact, the appointment of the President, and through his dependence on them, the virtual appointment to offices; among others the offices of the Judiciary Department. They are to make Treaties; and they are to try all impeachments. In allowing them thus to make the Executive & Judiciary appointments, to be the Court of impeachments, and to make Treaties which are to be laws of the land, the Legislative, Executive & Judiciary powers are all blended in one branch of the Government.

September 7.

Col: MASON said that in rejecting a Council to the President we were about to try an experiment on which the most despotic Governments had never ventured. The Grand Signor himself had his Divan. He moved to postpone the consideration of the clause in order to take up the following:

"That it be an instruction to the Committee of the States to prepare a clause or clauses for establishing an Executive Council, as a Council of State, for the President of the U. States, to consist of six members, two of which from the Eastern, two from the middle, and two from the Southern States, with a Rotation and duration of office similar to those of the Senate; such Council to be appointed by the Legislature or by the Senate."

September 8.

A Committee was then appointed by Ballot to revise the stile of and arrange the articles which had been agreed to by the House. The committee consisted of Mr. Johnson, Mr. Hamilton, Mr. Govr. Morris, Mr. Madison and Mr. King.

September 15.

Col: MASON 2ded. & followed Mr. Randolph in animadversions on the dangerous power and structure of the

Government, concluding that it would end either in monarchy, or a tyrannical aristocracy; which, he was in doubt, but one or other, he was sure. This Constitution had been formed without the knowledge or idea of the people. A second Convention will know more of the sense of the people, and be able to provide a system more consonant to it. It was improper to say to the people, take this or nothing.

Mason's language for describing Madison's scheme, on September 15, "take this or nothing," went directly to the heart of Madison's duplicity in creating his constitution.

Madison cleverly presented only one alternative. The Articles of Confederation were not on the ballot.

The entire body of delegates, prior to the appointment of the Committee on Style, on September 8, had not reached agreement on the powers of the Presidency.

The Committee on Style, appointed 3 days before the Convention ended, never released the final clauses of Article II, on the Presidency to the delegates, before they voted on them, on September 17.

Just like the dishonest act of Morris in secretly neutering the states by inserting "We the People," and "More perfect union," without showing the preamble to the delegates, the Committee on Style's text of Article II had not been seen or approved by the delegates.

The committee's charge was merely to put the Constitution into polished language. Morris left the vesting clause for the executive unaltered ("the executive Power shall be vested in a President of the United States of America"), but he changed the vesting clause for Congress to read: All legislative Powers herein granted shall be vested in a Congress of the United States" (emphasis added).

Rogue presidents could later claim that the different phrasing of the two branches' vesting clauses implies that there are executive powers beyond those "herein granted."

As Richard Nixon would explain, after his resignation, "when a President does it, it is not illegal."

In a contemporary example of Aristotle's definition of corruption, Hillary is beyond the rule of law. Obama is beyond the rule of law. In Madison's conception of rights, laws made by the elites apply to the non-elites.

The delegates never addressed the end goals to which the power of the president would be directed.

Mason and Wilson were exactly right in their prediction that Madison's plan would create an aristocratic tyranny of rogue presidents. Both delegates saw through Madison's sham "separation of powers and checks and balances."

The obvious flaw in Madison's separation of powers was that when the President, Congress, and Supreme Court are from the same political party, there is a unified, consolidated central power that does not derive its just powers from the consent of the governed.

There is no separation of power because all the branches think and act alike, unified by a common ideology.

The rogue President bends the law to his own political agenda, the Congress, of the same political party, then fails to restrain the rogue President, and the Supreme Court, of the same political party, rules that the President's actions are constitutional.

Mason stated that,

> Considering the powers of the President & those of the Senate, if a coalition should be established between

these two branches, they will be able to subvert the Constitution.

The obvious coalition was a political coalition in the three branches that was unified by political ideology.

Wilson added,

> They are to make Treaties; and they are to try all impeachments. In allowing them thus to make the Executive & Judiciary appointments, to be the Court of impeachments, and to make Treaties which are to be laws of the land, the Legislative, Executive & Judiciary powers are all blended in one branch of the Government.

On September 17, the last day of the Convention, Madison played the "We, the people," card for the first time against the natural rights populists, who supported sovereignty of the states.

Mason and Elbridge Gerry had moved for a committee to prepare a bill of rights to attach to Madison's document.

The motion was defeated by a vote of 10 to 0.

By September 17, only 10 states were in attendance. Many of the delegates in opposition to "We, the people" had already left the Convention, which is why only 37 of the initial 55 "We, the people" delegates signed the document, on September 17.

In the debate about the Bill of Rights, Madison stuck to his earlier arguments that a Bill of Rights was not needed because the state constitutions contained their own Bill of rights.

Two years later, he later changed his mind, and said that the Bill of Rights was needed.

In speaking against Mason's motion in the Bill of Rights, Roger Sherman stated that the reason that a Bill of Rights was not needed, was that,

> the State Declarations of Rights are not repealed by this Constitution and, being in force, are sufficient.

But, of course, it was not the states that created the Constitution, it was "We, the people."

"We, the people," was a national consolidated government that overrode the constitutions of the states, because "We, the people" was the supreme law of the land.

The rights in each state constitution had no significance in the national government. As Gouverneur Morris stated, on July 23,

> The Ellsworth amendment erroneously supposes that we are proceeding on the basis of the Confederation. This Convention is unknown to the Confederation.

For many decades, after the tenure of Andrew Jackson, the Presidents were more passive, and acted as administrators. This leadership style provided political stability for the nation because it was suited to Madison's Virginia Plan.

Beginning with Franklin Roosevelt, the stability of the American political system eroded because Roosevelt was never constrained in his socialist mission by the other branches of government.

At least Roosevelt believed in the sovereignty of the nation.

The series of rogue presidents, beginning with Lyndon Johnson, put the nation on the path to a centralized tyranny that was both disconnected from the consent of the governed, and shared no allegiance to the sovereignty of the United States.

In 2008, when Obama converted the Democrat Party into a global socialist party, the last vestiges of Madison's British two social class system evaporated.

No political party represented the financial interests of the working class, and both parties collaborated on converting the nation to a globalist nation, one among many.

President Adam's explanation was exactly right. There was no public purpose of protecting the natural rights of citizens in Madison's constitution.

"The reason," noted Adams,

> is that we have no Americans in America. The Nationalists have been no more Americans than the anties...Jefferson had a party. Hamilton had a party, but the commonwealth had none.

Patrick Henry was another natural rights patriot who saw through Madison's ruse about checks and balances.

During Virginia's ratifying convention, Henry wrote:

> Tell me not of checks on paper; but tell me of checks founded on self-love." The people's liberties are less safe under the proposed Constitution than under the British monarchy, for there at least the hereditary nobility have a stake in maintaining a balance between king and Commons; their continued existence depends on it. What corresponding incentives did the American analogues possess?

In the same Virginia convention, James Monroe cited the differences between the authentic British social class system and the truncated version that Madison created.

Monroe wrote:

> The English constitution is based upon social orders which have a repellent quality which enabled it to preserve itself from being destroyed by the other. The American division of power had no such basis and, indeed, no such intention. There are no real checks in the Constitution that would prevent a coalition of the branches of government and encroachments on the rights of the people.

Mason wrote,

> We are not indeed constituting a British Government, but a more dangerous monarchy, an elective one.

Madison played both sides of the issue. Sometimes, he acted like a patriot who was concerned about natural rights, and sometimes he was a Federalist, intent on creating a centralized government.

In 1785, Madison was in his natural rights mode, and wrote,

> The preservation of a free government requires not merely that the metes and bounds which separate each department of power be universally maintained but more especially that neither of them be suffered to overleap the great barrier which defends the rights of the people. The rulers who are guilty of such an encroachment exceed the commission from which they derive their authority and are tyrants. The people who submit to it are governed by laws made neither by themselves nor by an authority derived from them and are slaves.

In Federalist #39, he was still using the states rights side of the debate as a ruse to win support for his consolidated centralized scheme.

Madison wrote,

> The ratification of the Constitution was the assent of the people, but not as individuals composing one entire nation, but as composing the distinct and independent states to which they respectively belong. The ratification of the Constitution will not be a national act, but a federal act.

In 1787, Madison switched to his federalist mode. He was well aware that a government that did not protect the natural rights of citizens would end up with citizens being slaves to the government.

Madison then proceeded to draft his Virginia Plan that ended up making citizens slaves to the deep state.

Madison deliberately omitted the goal of his constitution, and deliberately failed to address the role of political parties in unifying all three branches of government.

By the time of the Kentucky Resolutions, Madison could clearly see the drift towards centralized tyranny.

In election of 1800, secret meetings of elites had begun selecting their party's presidential candidate. The newly elected President owed his allegiance to the elites who selected him, and to the political party apparatus that won the vote.

This closed, secret system of selecting candidates was called "King Caucus." The system made the President dependent on the political party.

As long as one party represented the interests of common citizens, and the other party represented the natural aristocracy, Madison's version of the British two-class, two-party, first-past-the-post election system, provided a modicum of political stability.

John Adams predicted the outcome by noting that the constitutional rules would divide the nation into two groups, creditors and debtors.

According to Adams, the purpose of Madison's constitution was to

> ...settle wealth and power upon a minority. It will be accomplished by a national debt, paper corporations, and offices, civil and military. These will condense king, lords and commons, a monied faction and an armed faction in one interest.

Beginning with President Johnson, presidents began using the CIA and FBI to undermine foreign governments, engage in secret wars and conduct espionage on U. S. citizens.

Following the prediction of President Adams, the deployment of the CIA was in the service of the wealthy elite.

President Johnson outlined his "Mann Doctrine," in 1964, that the U. S. foreign policy of overthrowing foreign democracies was based upon protecting the financial interests of U. S. corporations.

Johnson then proceeded to use the CIA to overthrow the elected governments in Brazil, (1964), Dominican Republic, (1965), Greece, (1965), Indonesia, (1965), and overtly lied to the American citizens about the illegal war in Viet Nam.

Following Johnson, President Nixon used the CIA to overthrow the government of Chile, (1970), and began the coup in Argentina, (1976).

In 1964, in the ramp up to the current deep state espionage on U. S. citizens, Johnson unleashed the FBI and the CIA on both black natural rights advocates and anti-war activists. Johnson thought both political movements were inspired by the same communist forces he was at war with in Viet Nam.

Johnson's use of the Office of President to spy on U. S. citizens was not prohibited by Madison's constitution, and the majority Democrats in Congress did not use their power to rein in the rogue President.

Nixon conducted a secret war in Cambodia, and bombed parts of Laos and Viet Nam into oblivion.

Congress did nothing to rein in the rogue President.

After Nixon conducted his illegal espionage on the Democrats, and had resigned, President Ford pardoned him, in a move consistent with how the earlier Federalists protected each other, and how today's elites protect their illicit privileges.

Madison's constitution allows the President the power to grant pardons, without any rules on the justification for the pardon.

Jimmy Carter joined the Tri-Lateral Commission in 1976, a secret global cabal of wealthy elites, whose mission is to coordinate bank monetary policy and financial transactions around the world.

The Tri-Lateral Commission marks the beginning of the shift in allegiance of the elites in the swamp from American sovereignty to a global governmental sovereignty.

In 1981, Reagan conducted an illegal war in El Salvador, to overthrow the democratically-elected government. Reagan's Contras were successful in killing 70,000 civilians.

Reagan placed a U. S. Navy blockade of Nicaragua, and mined their harbors.

Congress did nothing.

Reagan ignored Congress about funding the Contras, and began using arms sales to Iran to fund his war in Nicaragua. When he was caught lying to the American people, and violating the law, Congress did nothing to rein in the rogue President.

In 1983, Reagan invaded Grenada to overthrow the government there.

Reagan conducted an illegal, secret war in Afganistan, and funded Muslim terrorist groups. One of those terrorists, Osama Bin Laden, eventually used the resources provided by Reagan to bomb New York in 2001.

In 1989, Bush sent 120,000 U. S. troops to invade Panama, to overthrow the dictatorship of Noreiga. The ostensible, public lie used by Bush to justify the invasion was "war on drugs." His actions were not authorized by Congress and violated the 1973 War Powers Act.

Congress did nothing.

In the first explicit reference to the deep state globalist ambitions of the Republican Party, Bush proclaimed a "New World Order," in 1991.

The new world order was based upon the military power of the U. S. to protect the financial interests of global corporations.

In 2003, Bush sent 250,000 U. S. troops to invade Iraq. Opponents of the invasion called it "War for Oil." More accurately, it could have been called New World Order war because Bush had laid out plans to invade 5 other countries.

The Bush "neo-con" cabal that managed the new world order was the beginning of today's deep state elites.

In 2002, as a part of the deep state management, Bush ordered the NSA to begin spying on U. S. citizens, and keeping computer records of suspected enemies of the new world order.

Bush justified his espionage on U. S. citizens by stating that he had absolute moral clarity to engage in illegal acts.

There is nothing in Madison's Constitution that reins in a rogue president, like Bush, from committing illegal acts.

As Nixon correctly observed, "when the President does it, it is not illegal."

There is nothing in Madison's checks and balances that limits the President because his acts are sanctioned by a political party, not by the Constitution.

When the 3 branches are all under one party, there are no institutional checks and balances against presidential tyranny.

The two historical forces that perpetuated the current deep state were the use of U. S. military power to overthrow foreign governments, and the use of the CIA and FBI to punish domestic citizens who opposed the rogue presidents.

Beginning around 2005, the corporate globalist ambitions of the Republicans began to merge in alliance with the global socialist ambitions of the Democrats.

Beginning with Obama, the two political parties began colluding on the implementation and management of the new world order.

Their collusion was facilitated by the unelected agents in the deep state.

Obama inherited the deep state apparatus created by Bush, and extended its effectiveness in undermining the sovereignty of the nation and the natural rights of citizens.

In the absence of explicitly stating that liberty was the end goal for government, Madison's constitution did not yoke his assumption about the "virtue" of the natural aristocracy to the social cultural values that bind citizens together in the patriotic common cause of liberty.

In contrast to Madison's philosophically vacuous "more perfect union," in Obama's socialism, Marxian class war, socialist ideology, and white privilege within the capitalist legal system, constitute the context for creating a "more perfect union."

Obama's job, as he defined it, was to redistribute the income that existed from the globalist economy to correct his idea of the unfair distribution of wealth.

His allegiance to the American rule of law is subordinated to his higher allegiance to his religion of global socialism.

Obama has no allegiance to the rule of law because he despises the principles upon which the American government are based.

The deployment of the FBI was intended, by Obama, to force obedience to the rule of law in socialism, in strict adherence to what Obama determined it to be, at any moment in time.

In their logic, the socialists, like Obama, are absolutely certain that their policies lead to greater social welfare and social justice, than the individualistic logic of the natural rights republic. Like Bush, Obama had absolute moral certainty about the benefits of global socialism.

There is nothing in Madison's constitution that prohibits a rogue president, like Obama, from pursuing the socialist ideology.

Obama knew that once citizens give up their natural rights in exchange for government welfare, the socialists would be able control the citizens for life, by controlling the ideology of socialist class hatred.

The socialists in Obama's lawless regime, across all branches of government, were united by this common ideology. This type of unified ideological interest in the 3 branches of government is contrary to Madison's principles of separation of power.

Obama's regime was organized, state-sanctioned lawlessness, designed to impose a socialist dictatorship. Obama used the deep-state apparatus, created by Bush to conduct a series of criminal acts.

April 2009: Obama leaks the unmasked name of Congresswoman Jane Harmon to the press. According to news reports, the Bush administration NSA incidentally recorded and saved Harmon's phone conversations with pro-Israel lobbyists who were under investigation for espionage.

2010: The IRS secretly begins "targeting" conservative groups that are seeking nonprofit tax-exempt status, by singling out ones that have "Tea Party" or "Patriot" in their names.

Army intelligence analyst Bradley Manning begins illegally leaks classified information to WikiLeaks revealing, among other matters, that the U.S. is extensively spying on the United Nations.

Obama Attorney General Eric Holder renews a Bush-era subpoena of New York Times reporter James Risen in a leak investigation.

Obama administration pursues espionage charges against NSA whistleblower Thomas Drake. The judge called the government's conduct in the case "unconscionable."

May 28, 2010: The government secretly applies for a warrant to obtain Google email information of Fox News reporter James Rosen in a leak investigation, without telling Rosen.

Summer 2016: The FBI reportedly obtains a secret FISA court order to monitor communications of Trump adviser Carter

Page, convincing a judge there's probable cause to believe Page is acting as a Russian agent.

CNN later reports that the Obama Justice Department wiretapped Trump campaign manager Paul Manafort before the 2016 election over Russia ties, and continued it through the early part of 2017.

Fall 2016: Trump opponents "shop" to reporters a political opposition research "dossier" alleging Trump is guilty of various inappropriate acts regarding Russia. A copy of the report is provided to the FBI.

September 26, 2016: It's not publicly known at the time, but the government makes a proposal to the secretive Foreign Intelligence Surveillance Court (FISC) court to allow the National Counter Terrorism Center to access "unmasked" intel on Americans acquired by the FBI and NSA.

October 26, 2016: At a closed-door hearing before the Foreign Intelligence Surveillance Court, the Obama administration disclosed that it had been violating surveillance laws. It disclosed that more than 5 percent of its searches of the NSA's database violated the law.

November 2016-January 2017: News reports claim Rice's interest in the NSA materials accelerates after President Trump's election through his January inauguration. Surveillance reportedly included Trump transition figures and foreign officials discussing a Trump administration.

December 2016: FBI secretly monitors and records communications between the Russian ambassador, and Lt. Gen. Michael Flynn. After Trump's election, Obama officials take steps to ensure certain intelligence gathered regarding Trump associates is "spread across the government." One Obama official would later say it's because they were afraid once Trump officials "found out how we knew what we knew," the intelligence would be destroyed."

December 15, 2016: National Security Adviser Susan Rice acknowledged that the Obama administration spied on Trump officials in Trump Tower, but claimed it was incidental to the administration's spying on the foreign leader, the UAE crown prince. Rice admitted to "unmasking" the names of the Trump officials who met with the crown prince, saying it was important to know who they were, although the identities of Americans are supposed to be strictly protected.

January 10, 2017: The socialist propaganda media reports on the veracity of the Trump "dossier" as authentic.

January 12, 2017: The Obama administration finalizes new rules allowing the National Security Agency (NSA) to spread certain intelligence to 16 other U.S. intel agencies without the normal privacy protections.

February 2, 2017: The media reports that five information technology (IT) computer professionals employed by Democrats in the House of Representatives are under criminal investigation for allegedly "accessing House IT systems without lawmakers' knowledge." The suspects include three brothers, "who managed office information technology for members of the House Permanent Select Committee on Intelligence and other lawmakers."

February 9, 2017: News of the FBI recordings of Lt. Gen. Flynn speaking with Russia's ambassador is leaked to the press. The New York Times and the Washington Post report that Flynn's dialogue was captured on wiretaps.

March 20, 2017: At a hearing, lead House Intelligence Committee Democrat Adam Schiff places Trump adviser Carter Page at the center of a theoretical alleged collusion with Russia. Schiff's statement is the Democrat's coordinated attempt with the socialist media to establish public justification for the Obama administration intel community's controversial surveillance of the Trump adviser during the 2016 political campaign.

The espionage Obama and Rice conducted during the Trump transition was different than the routine criminal spying, before the inauguration. Prior to the election, Obama used the deep state agents to punish his enemies.

During the transition, Obama intended to use the deep state to subvert the American judicial and election process, in order to stop Trump's inauguration.

In other words, Obama was deploying the FBI to initiate a coup d'etate.

The explanation of why there was never any opposition from the Republicans, or from the system of checks and balances in Madison's constitution, is that his constitution never stated the mission of the Office of President.

Neither political party defends the public purpose of individual liberty, and all branches of government are committed to a global government.

A rogue president, like Obama, can easily subvert Madison's constitutional rules, without legal consequence.

Madison's flawed document suffered from two debilitating defects.

It was an illegitimate, illegal attempt to subvert the Articles and it was never ratified by the citizens in an open honest fair election.

Madison played both sides of the issue on the correct process for ratifying his constitution.

At first, he was in favor of a citizen's referendum. He explained his reasoning in his letter to Jefferson, on March 19, 1787.

> I think myself that it will be expedient... to lay the foundation of the new system in such a ratification by the people themselves of the several States as will render it clearly paramount to their Legislative authorities.

One month later, Madison was still in his popular vote modality. On April 16, 1787, he explained to George Washington:

> To give the new system its proper validity and energy, a ratification must be obtained from the people, and not merely from the ordinary authority of the Legislatures.

Madison then reverted to his second method of ratifying his work, proposed in a series of non-public resolutions that he transmitted to the Congress of the government he was intending to overthrow.

Article VII of his constitution states only that 9 states were required to ratify the new constitution, not the 13 states required by the Articles.

His second method was a charade of citizen ratification. The 37 "We, the people," went home and had themselves selected as delegates in the fraudulent ratification conventions, where they easily manipulated the favorable outcome for the Federalists.

The new constitution of the Democratic Republic of America provides a detailed mission statement for the Office of President.

It is the constitutional duty of the President to preserve, protect and defend the natural and civil rights of citizens and to defend the sovereign borders of the nation from foreign and domestic threats.

The new Constitution codifies that the act of spying on citizens or conducting espionage against the sovereignty of citizens or the states is clearly defined as a felony and impeachable crime, not just limited to the President, but to all national employees.

Upon taking office, after the election, the President swears a two-part oath. The first part is to recite part of the Declaration of Independence.

> When in the Course of human events it becomes necessary for one people to dissolve the political bands which have connected them with another and to assume among the powers of the earth, the separate and equal station to which the Laws of Nature and of Nature's God entitle them, a decent respect to the opinions of mankind requires that they should declare the causes which impel them to the separation.
>
> I hold these truths to be self-evident, that all men are created equal, that they are endowed by their Creator with certain unalienable Rights, that among these are Life, Liberty and the pursuit of Happiness. That to secure these rights, Governments are instituted among Men, deriving their just powers from the consent of the governed, That whenever any Form of Government becomes destructive of these ends, it is the Right of the People to alter or to abolish it, and to institute new Government, laying its foundation on such principles and organizing its powers in such form, as to them shall seem most likely to effect their Safety and Happiness.

Upon the conclusion of reciting the Declaration, The President swears the following oath of office:

> I do solemnly swear that I will faithfully execute the Office of President of the Democratic Republic of America, according to the principles of government

stated in the Constitution of the Democratic Republic of America.

I solemnly swear to preserve, protect and defend the natural and civil rights of citizens and to defend the sovereign borders of the nation from foreign and domestic threats.

So Help me, God.

Article II, The Office of President, in the new Constitution of the Democratic Republic of America corrects the defects in Madison's flawed document. The first improvement concerns term limits.

Section 1.

The executive power of the National Government shall be vested in a President of the Democratic Republic of America. He shall hold his office for a term of four years, and, may serve a second term, if elected.

No President may serve more than two terms, and no more than 10 years during a lifetime.

The new constitution clarifies the election process for the President, and shortens the duration of time from the election, in November, to the inauguration, on December 1.

No Person except a natural born citizen, or a verified Citizen of the Democratic Republic of America for the previous 10 years, shall be eligible for election of President; The President must be at least 35 years of age on the date of assuming office.

The President selects the candidate of Vice President, no later than August 1, of the year of the Presidential election.

The national election for President is held during the two days of the first weekend in November.

The presidential candidate with a majority of electoral college votes is declared the winner, by the House of Representatives, no later than November 15 of the year of the election. The number of electors for each State is equal to the whole number of Senators and Representatives to which the State may be entitled in the Congress.

The Electors shall meet in their respective States, and are legally obligated to vote according to the popular vote of the citizens.

The term of office for the President begins December 1 of the year of the election.

The new constitution improves the convoluted rules in Madison's constitution on the process of removing the President.

In case of the removal of the President from Office, or of his death, resignation, or inability to discharge the powers and duties of the Office, the Vice President assumes the office of President, no later than 24 hours after the removal of the President.

The House of Representatives, by law, may provide for the designation of an interim President, in the event that both the President and Vice President are not able to serve the Office. Within 24 hours of appointing an interim President, the House of Representatives shall set the time and conditions of the election of a new President, by a vote of valid citizens in each state, to be held within 30 days of the appointment of the interim President.

The President, Vice President, and all civil officers whose appointment to office is confirmed by the National Congress, shall be subject to impeachment for treason against the sovereign interests of the nation or the sovereign interests of the states, espionage against verified citizens, bribery by a foreign government, or other national felony.

The new constitution limits the authority of the President to conduct illegal wars.

The President shall be the Supreme Commander in Chief of all military personnel and resources

Upon a presentment of a declaration of war by the President, the National Congress shall have the power to declare war and authorize the application of military power and action against foreign enemies, within 2 days of receiving the President's declaration. No military action undertaken by the President may continue after 48 hours, without the consent of the National Congress.

The President shall be the Supreme Commander in Chief of the Army and Navy of the Democratic Republic, and of the National Guard of the several States, when called into the actual service of the Democratic Republic; he may require the opinion, in writing, of the principal officer in each of the military departments, upon any subject relating to the duties of their respective offices. The opinions and reports shall be public records and documents, released to the public within 48 hours.

The new constitution clarifies the division of power between the President and the National Congress.

The President shall have power to grant reprieves and pardons for offences against the Democratic Republic of America, except in cases of impeachment of any national official.

The President shall have power, by and with the advice and consent of the Senate, to make treaties, provided two thirds of the Senators present concur; and he shall nominate, and by and with the advice and consent of the Senate, appoint ambassadors, other public ministers and consuls, and all other Executive Officers of the Democratic Republic of America, whose appointments are not herein otherwise provided for, and which shall be established by law: but the Congress may by law vest the appointment of such inferior officers, as they think proper, in the President alone, in the executive officers of the executive departments.

The President shall have the power to fill all executive vacancies that may happen during the recess of the National Congress, by granting commissions which shall expire at the resumption of the session of the National Congress.

He shall, on January 21 of each year, present to the National Congress, the State of the Union, and recommend to their consideration such measures as he shall judge necessary and expedient for the next two years, including his proposal for the two year budget of the Democratic Republic of America.

Conclusion:

During the North Carolina ratifying convention, Delegate Lenoir stated,

> This constitution is not proper for our adoption, as I consider that it endangers our liberties. ..The president has great powers. There is no assurance of the liberty of the press. They have power to control our elections…Its powers are very indefinite.

North Carolina was the only state to veto the constitution on philosophical issues about individual freedom.

Jefferson cited North Carolina's opposition, in his letter of March 23, 1789, to John Paul Jones,

> North Carolina insists that the amendments should be made before she would accede…This security for liberty seems to be demanded by the general voice of America.

At least the North Carolina convention was not a farce like proceedings in Delaware and Georgia, whose self-selected elites approved the constitution in several days, with little public notice and superficial debate.

Madison admitted in Federalist #40 that the ratification process was a fraud. Madison argued that just because the ratification process was a fraud, that was not a reason to veto the constitution.

Madison stated,

> Or if there be a man whose propensity to condemn is susceptible of no control, let me then ask what sentence he has in reserve for the twelve States who USURPED THE POWER of sending deputies to the convention, a body utterly unknown to their constitutions; for Congress, who recommended the appointment of this body, equally unknown to the Confederation; and for the State of New York, in particular, which first urged and then complied with this unauthorized interposition? But that the objectors may be disarmed of every pretext, it shall be granted for a moment that the convention were neither authorized by their commission, nor justified by circumstances in proposing a Constitution for their country: does it follow that the Constitution ought, for that reason alone, to be rejected? If, according to the noble precept, it be lawful to accept good advice even from an enemy, shall we set the ignoble example of refusing such advice even when it is offered by our friends?

The British model concocted by Madison was an abject failure in preventing centralized tyranny because the British model does not have a president.

It has a prime minister, who reports to the King.

The Office of President, in Madison's system, became an unguided missile of rogue Presidents, who like Bush and

Obama, claimed absolute moral authority to subvert the constitution that they had sworn to uphold and defend.

Chapter 7.
Eliminating Corporate Corruption In the Natural Rights Republic.

Madison's American version of the British Constitution was influenced by the legal philosophy of Sir William Blackstone, who wrote Commentaries on the Laws of England.

Because the United Kingdom was a monarchy, Blackstone spent a great deal of his book explaining how the king acted as a non-elected counter-balance to the British Parliament.

Blackstone wrote,

> The king is himself a part of the parliament: and, as this is the reason of his being so, very properly therefore the share of legislation, which the constitution has placed in the crown, consists in the power of rejecting, rather than resolving.

The term used to describe the king's role in checking the power of Parliament was "Crown-in-Parliament." Blackstone wrote, "Crown in Parliament was sovereign in all matters of concern to the British empire."

After 1687, part of the king's constitutional authority was assumed in the parliament's implementation of the prerogatives of the crown.

The king's responsibility was to act as the ultimate supreme authority in British law to overrule unconstitutional acts of the Parliament.

The king's agent in Parliament was the Prime Minister, who the king appointed.

Under the unwritten British constitution, the power of Parliament was not balanced within the institutions and agencies of government. It was balanced by the Crown in

Parliament, operating outside the agencies of government, to compel obedience to the rule of law.

Blackstone wrote,

> If the Parliament of Great Britain will positively enact a thing to be done, which is unreasonable, I know of no power in the ordinary forms of the British Constitution that is vested with authority to control it.

In other words, there is no force inside the institutional framework of the British Parliament that acts to control the actions of the Parliament.

The final, supreme arbiter of power in Great Britain is the king.

If Madison had followed Blackstone's British contract law, Madison's central government would have been an agent of 13 state principals.

Madison eliminated the basis of the British principal-agency relationship and substituted his own version of the balance of power.

As was the case in creating the Office of President, the fit between the British constitution and Madison's constitution was not perfect.

Madison inverted the balance of power by making one of the branches of government, the Supreme Court, the ultimate judge of its own powers, and also of the powers of the Congress, the President, and the states.

To summarize, in the case of the Office of President, Madison relied on his own version of the British prime minister for his concept of the American president.

In his concept of balanced power, Madison substituted the Supreme Court as the sole arbiter of government power, as if the Supreme Court was the Crown-in-Parliament.

When the King surrendered to the states, in Paris in 1783, he wrote,

> His Brittanic Majesty acknowledges the said United States to be free, sovereign and independent States.

The King surrendered to 13 states, not to "We, the people."

Madison did not accept the surrender of the King as establishing the sovereignty of states. The terms used by the King would have forced Madison to admit that the 13 states had 13 individual principle-agency contracts with the King.

If Madison had accepted the independent sovereignty of the states, he could not have used his ruse of "We, the people."

Without his ruse of "We, the people," Madison would not have been able to implement his version of the balance of power.

The balance of power was not an equal sharing of power between the two social class "factions." Madison's balance was a permanent balance that elevated the financial interests of the elite above the financial interests of the common class.

In his attempt to evade the sovereignty of states, Madison had to ignore 3 founding documents of the new nation, and he had to implement his balance of power without relying on Locke's compact theory of government.

The three historical documents that Madison had to evade in his new formula of balanced power had stipulated that the 13 states had formed a contract to establish the new nation.

- The Declaration of Independence.
- The Articles of Confederation.

- The Treaty of Paris.

In the first instance, Madison's new formula sought to balance the institutional powers of the three branches of government, without mentioning the Declaration of Independence.

Second, he sought to balance power between the new central government and the states, without mentioning the Articles of Confederation.

Third, he sought to use constitutional rules to elevate the financial interests of the natural aristocracy over the common class, without mentioning that the natural aristocracy in America was just like the nobility of Great Britain.

All three forces were interrelated and each political force affected the other forces in Madison's scheme.

Under the Articles of Confederation, it was common for a state to pass legislation that granted debt relief to farmers.

Granting debt relief to the common class was not supportive of elite financial interests, and Madison sought to prevent the states from enacting debt relief for farmers with the Contracts Clause, and the sovereignty of the Supreme Court to interpret the law.

In conjunction with the Contracts Clause, Madison's Constitution prohibited states from issuing their own paper money and from regulating the banking affairs of the central government.

In both Madison and Hamilton, the Constitution defines bills of credit to signify a paper medium of exchange intended to circulate, like money, between individuals, and between the Government and individuals, for the ordinary purposes of economic transactions.

States issued bills of credit to pay for government expenses. The Constitution forbid states from issuing bills of credit because they were not "legal tender," as defined by the Constitution.

As a part of cementing the privileges of the natural aristocracy, Marshall ruled that when, and where, either the state, or Federal government, received state bank notes in payment and discharge of an execution, (Contracts Clause), the creditor (natural aristocracy), was entitled to demand payment in gold or silver, (Commerce Clause).

Natural rights conservatives, in 1787, correctly diagnosed Madison's flawed concept of the balance of power, both within the 3 branches, between the two social classes, and also between the federal government and the states.

John Taylor of Caroline, in his analysis of Madison's constitution, titled, Construction Construed and Constitutions Vindicated, wrote,

> when the constitution operates upon collisions between political departments, it is not to be construed by the courts. To allow the Supreme Court to be the arbiter of its own powers perverts the very idea of compact.

Eight years into the new Constitution, the consequences of Madison's flawed concept of his balance of power became more evident. The financial power of the elites had translated into a political power of incipient elite tyranny.

The Kentucky Resolves, of 1798, stated,

> the Constitution is a compact and each state acceded as a state. The central government should not be the exclusive or final judge of its own powers.

As he did throughout his life, Madison played both sides of the argument about the balance of power.

He wrote Article III, of the Constitution, which made the Supreme Court the ultimate judge of all laws, and he also wrote the Kentucky Resolves, which stated that the Supreme Court should not be the final judge of its own powers.

As a consequence of the way Madison balanced the 3 powers, the nation devolved into a special financial interest driven system whose operational logic was fueled by elite corruption.

Special interest legislation and special interest lobbyists used the agencies of government to extract financial benefits for their clients.

Eventually, the power of the natural aristocracy evolved into global corporate power, and that corporate corruption fuels the agents in the deep state today.

Aristotle, the third-century B. C. Greek philosopher, defined corruption as the practice of leaders who ruled with a view to their private advantage rather than the pursuit of the public interest.

Aristotle also viewed the 3 possible forms of government as the one, the few, and the many.

In his classification of the few, Aristotle described how it ended in corruption because the aristocracy used the government for their own financial enrichment.

Aristotle described the end of political society, as a result of elite corruption in the second classification of government by the few.

Polybius, another Greek philosopher, used the same government classification system as Aristotle.

Unlike the end of society, as described by Aristotle, Polybius thought that the phase of aristocracy would be replaced by the democracy of the many.

His term for democracy of the many was Democratic Republic.

America is currently in the phase of government described as a corrupt aristocracy. The corruption is endemic and epidemic.

The government and private sector corruption infects every aspect of American society

But, Madison feared the democracy of the many, and his constitution truncated democratic procedures because of his fear that common citizens (the many) may oppress the natural aristocracy (the few).

In Madison's rule of law, the cultural value of shared individual liberty, in the Declaration, was replaced with the British class cultural value of shared plunder.

Shared plunder ended up as corruption.

Madison's rules substituted a principle of shared plunder and greed to exploit the system for the rule of law in the Articles of Confederation, which were based upon a shared cultural sense of fairness and citizen patriotism.

As described by Robert Horowitz, in The Moral Foundations of the American Republic, Madison thought that if the common class could develop a class consciousness, that the common citizens would not devolve into a dangerous "faction," one of Madison's favorite terms to describe social class competition.

According to Horowitz, Madison thought that,

> If all citizens (working class) have the same impulse of passion and interest (as the elites), they would not divide into oppressive and dangerous factions… if (working class) Americans can be made to divide themselves according to their narrow economic interests they will avoid the fatal factionalism.

Madison's constitution provided the institutional separation of power that divided the working class into their narrow economic (class) interests.

His logic was that if both social classes shared the moral value of shared plunder, then the common class would not use democratic procedures to impose their majority views on the virtuous elites.

But, Madison's concept of balance was skewed against the common citizens and Madison provided no safety valve for the common citizens to protect themselves when the system devolved into a corrupt corporate tyranny.

Madison's rules of economic exchange established the constitutional basis of centralized corporate corruption, by the empowered aristocracy.

The unchecked power of the Federal government over banking and money, created a national economy based upon periodic financial panics and economic collapse.

The economic instability is caused by the elite's unchecked power over banking and money.

Hamilton created the First Bank as a private-for-profit corporation, that was not subject to state taxes. As a private corporation, the contracts and activities of the Bank were protected from interference, by either the states or the federal government, by the Contracts Clause.

Madison inserted the Contracts Clause so that a State would not be allowed to pass any law that "impairs the obligation of contracts."

As a compliment to the Contracts Clause in solidifying the balance of power, Justice Marshall ruled that the Federal government, under the necessary and proper clause, could create any type of financial corporation that could possibly be seen to promote the "general welfare."

Hamilton wrote to Washington, in 1791,

> Every power vested in Government is in its nature sovereign and includes by force of the term a right to employ all means requisite and fairly applicable to the attainment of such power.

Justice Marshall, in his ruling on McCullough vs. Maryland (1819), re-stated Hamilton's words, almost verbatim,

> Let the end be legitimate, let it be within the scope of the constitution, and all means which are appropriate are constitutional.

The government, in other words, had become Leviathan. In its modern incarnation, Leviathan is the same as global corporatism, that uses the agencies of government for its own purpose.

Hamilton knew exactly what the role of corruption would be in maintaining elite control over economic policy.

Hamilton stated, in his 1792 dinner with Jefferson that,

> Purge the Government of its corruption and give to its popular branch equality of representation and it would become an impracticable government.

The power of corruption in perpetuating elite control over economic affairs was to permanently elevate the rights of creditors over debtors, and to require that all contracts be paid in gold and silver.

President Jackson stated, in 1832, that Hamilton's Bank "makes the rich richer, and prostituted the government to the advancement of the few at the expense of the many."

President Martin VanBuren, in 1837, stated that the constitution must be amended to "stop blending private interests with the operations of public business."

The most common form of corporate corruption was the use of government revenues to benefit private projects and real estate interests.

John Calhoun's Federal legislation for internal improvements justified the power of government to appropriate revenues for private projects, as long as the project served "the general welfare and common defense."

South Carolina Governor John Wilson, in 1822, correctly diagnosed that the doctrine of implied powers served to benefit the elites. Wilson wrote, "The friends of assumed powers (elites) regarding internal improvements claim the powers as implied."

From the 1830's onward, special financial privileges were built into every Federal program, leading to the power and influence of unelected lobbyists.

Over time, the influence of the lobbyists grew, and as that influence grew, the interests of common citizens diminished, because they were not represented in Washington by lobbyists.

As the system of representation evolved into a special interest-driven political system, the concept of government protecting the natural rights of citizens disappeared.

In Madison's system there are no lobbyists or organized political parties designed to represent the public purpose of individual liberty.

Beginning with the Viet Nam military-industrial political machine, the domestic and foreign affairs of large corporations dominated public policy.

The military-industrial lobbyists were able to perpetuate the war in order to sell the government military supplies.

Unlike World War II, where the large American corporations benefited from trade with Hitler, Viet Nam was a sea change in U. S. corporate corruption.

The American corporations benefited from a war that they would not allow to end.

From the Viet Nam era, the corporations became less and less connected to the domestic interests of the nation, and more and more connected to the interests of a global, one-world government, that they controlled through their unelected agents in the deep-state and their network of global financial institutions.

One economic result of Madison's scheme is a continuous cycle of economic collapse. The financial and economic severity of the economic collapse has increased in frequency and intensity, since 1964.

The economic instability is caused by money growth, inflation and speculation in assets.

The source of corporate power is the ability of the elites to control the supply of money, (M2), and the Federal Reserve banking system, which operates just as Hamilton's First Bank did, as a private for-profit corporation, disconnected from the consent of the governed.

That type of private control over the nation's money and fiscal policies leads to a predictable cycle of economic collapse, about every 10 years.

The macro economic instability is caused first by a predictable sequence of events, beginning with a period of a rapid increase in money supply and an increase in fiscal spending and debt issuance.

The loose money policies cause a period of asset speculation and inflation.

The speculation leads to a gigantic bubble in assets and the creation of synthetic investment instruments, which then burst, causing aggregate demand to collapse and asset values to plummet.

In the period of the bubble burst, common citizens lose their houses and their farms to the elite, due to the way the creditor/debtor laws are written to benefit the bankers.

Bankers, and creditors, then proceed to foreclose on the property and assets of common citizens, who cannot make their debt payments.

During the period of asset speculation, the rate of private capital investment collapses, causing economic decline in the 3 to 5 year horizon, as capital is shifted from productive investments that lead to long-term capital gains, to investments in speculative assets in hopes of a short-term capital gain.

During the period of economic collapse, the common citizens become financially destitute, and seek welfare assistance from the government.

As predicted by President Jackson, the concentration of wealth, and the distribution of income, becomes more and more concentrated in the hands of the few.

Charles Beard argued in his 1913 book, An Economic Interpretation of the Constitution of the United States, that Madison assumed that elite commercial and financial interests were the primary forces that needed to be balanced against the non-elite social classes, in the three branches of government.

Beard showed that the 37 Founding Federalists all had a personal vested financial interest in skewing the results of the new constitutional rules to suit their own needs, while at the same time, attempting to ensure stability in the government by establishing rules of procedure that balanced financial factions against each other.

Madison's rules did not create a free enterprise competitive market.

As described by Beard, the elites created an unbalanced economy, directed by elites, who deployed their natural rights of property to gain unchecked power over the common citizens.

As Hamilton explained,

> all parts of society were of a piece, that all ranks and degrees were organically connected through a great chain in such a way that those on top were necessarily involved in the welfare of those below them.

For about the first 200 years of the nation, the tyranny by the elites led to economic collapse for common citizens about every 10 years.

The nation's banking system collapsed in 1813, as a result of the First Bank's corruption in speculative investments, and the mal-appropriation of Indian lands in Michigan and Ohio.

The banking system, and economy, collapsed again in 1819, as a result of the bank's securities becoming worthless.

Because European bankers owned securities issued by the 1st Bank, the collapse in America's banking system quickly spread to Europe, leading to an international financial collapse.

As a result of the collapse in 1819, the first wave of appropriation of farm land by the bankers occurred, as farm prices collapsed, and farmers could not pay their debts.

The Tariff of 1824, designed to protect northern financial interests, caused the wholesale price of cotton in the South to drop from 18 cents to 9 cents.

The Tariff of 1824 marked the first phase of the irreconcilable financial split between northern and southern elites, which culminated in the Civil War.

The U. S. banking system collapsed again, in 1836. As a consequence of this collapse, President Jackson was able to muster enough political support to kill the 2cd Bank.

Agricultural land and commodity prices collapsed in 1837, leading to the longest depression in U. S. history.

The 1837 collapse led to the second great wave of land appropriation by the elites, in conjunction with the land appropriation of Indian lands, after Jackson forcibly removed the Indians to Oklahoma.

During the financial panic of 1857, the bond notes issued by 1400 state banks became worthless. During this collapse, 5000 businesses failed, leading to the first wave of massive unemployment of common workers in U. S. metro regions.

In the aftermath of the Civil War, thousands of farmers lost their lands in the debt-peonage system, and were forced to work in the textile and tobacco industry, in an economic system called "neo-slavery."

In his book, The Mind of the South, C. Wright Mills correctly described this era as the re-establishment of the Plantation Aristocracy in the mills, achieved by brute force and racial apartheid.

Beginning with the 1987 stock market collapse, the cycle of economic instability became more frequent, and more intense.

Between 1985 and 1992, changes in tax and trade policies led to increased rates of American domestic production jobs lost due to offshoring and outsourcing.

The production that used to be done in the U. S. was now done in foreign locations. The beneficial economic flows, the so-called "trickle-down effect," in the American economy became concentrated in the top 15% of the population that was connected to the global trade patterns.

The other 85% of the population turned to the "gig" economy to survive.

As a result of the trade policies, the economic platform for U.S. technology R&D and new technology product development shifted to U. S. branch manufacturing plants in India and China.

On October 19, 1987, the Black Monday Stock Market Crash occurred. The cause of the crash was banking collusion with agents of the deep state, asset speculation, insider trading and program trading by 5 large global securities firms.

In 1991, the speculative real estate bubble, and the leveraged buy-out bubble, both burst at the same time, causing the recession of 1991.

Beginning in 1991, the American economy began to enter a series of speculative bubbles caused by government banking policy intervention, in its attempt to restore macro aggregate demand, through increased government spending.

As a result of the increased government spending, the frequency of economic collapse shortened from every 10 years to about every 5 years.

The capital gains and profits from the exits in IT investments, initially made in 1992, were ploughed back into short-term speculative early stage IPO investments, in 1997.

Speculation and collusion in the IPO market dumped hundreds of millions of worthless IT securities into the public markets for ordinary American investors to buy.

After the Islamic terrorist attack, on September 11, 2001, the U. S. economy entered a prolonged recession.

The U. S. government tried stimulus spending, which ended up primarily benefiting special financial interests in foreign counties.

In 2002, U. S. trade and tax policies were changed to facilitate more offshoring of technology innovation and R&D.

The changes in regulation of corporations led to a series of Enron-type collapses and wide-spread corporate financial accounting fraud.

In the period from 2003 to 2008, the U. S. rate of job creation was lower than the rate of job destruction.

Beginning in 2003, the U. S. rate of domestic direct investment declined, and U. S. foreign direct investment increased.

In 2004, the U. S. rates of profit for the 1500 largest global corporation increased to record levels. As a result of U. S. trade and tax policies, those record profits were not repatriated, or reinvested, in U. S. domestic value chains. The record profits were reinvested in foreign global value chains.

Beginning in March, 2008, speculation in oil and gas increased the price of a barrel of oil from $43 per barrel to $145 per barrel.

The asset speculation was a result of collusion between oil corporations and government officials, aided and abetted by a useless war in Iraq and Afganistan.

The rapid increase in oil prices caused a sharp contraction in consumer spending. The decreased consumer spending caused aggregate demand to collapse, causing a prolonged economic recession.

In September 2008, the mortgage debt bubble, directly caused by U. S. government banking and interest rate policies, burst, and the U. S. economy collapsed again.

As a result of that collapse, and coincident with the election of a socialist president, the U. S. economy did not experience growth for the next 8 years.

In the absence of economic growth, between 2008 to 2016, citizens became attracted to the ideology of socialism, which resulted in 65 million citizens voting for the socialist candidate for President, in 2016.

Eliminating corruption in the natural rights republic means eliminating the source of corrupt power in Madison's Constitution.

The source of corruption is the elite's control over the banking and monetary system.

The aristocratic American government created by Madison was politically stable as long as the well born created economic growth.

There is an obvious economic relationship between individual freedom and economic growth, commonly called the competitive free market.

The economic growth is caused by Locke's right of private property, which unleashes individual initiative and ingenuity. The common phrase for that individualist ideology was "Yankee ingenuity."

What Madison overthrew, in 1787, was the voluntary exchange economy of the Articles of Confederation, where common citizens could freely gain the value of their labor (property).

Madison replaced the Articles, which were based upon equal commercial exchanges, with government rules, where the elites dominated the terms of exchange with their unbalanced, and unchecked government power.

Madison unleashed a perpetual class war in America between the elites and the non-elites.

The corruption of his system is exactly as predicted by Aristotle, an aristocracy that ended in corruption.

The first check against corrupt tyranny in the Democratic Republic of America is to place the issuance of charters under the consent of the governed. Because the House represents the interests of citizens, the House gains the constitutional power to regulate trade practices.

The House has the exclusive authority to regulate the issuance of charters for interstate and international commerce. The House may impose restrictions, sanctions and revocations of charters for trade practices that are contrary to the sovereignty and welfare of citizens or the states.

The second barrier to corrupt tyranny is to revoke the ability of the elites to borrow money to increase government spending.

The National Congress shall have the power to issue government bonds, and to borrow money on the credit of the Democratic Republic of America. All proposals to borrow money or issue debt shall occur once in the two year budget cycle, and all proposals to issue debt must be approved by 50% of the State legislatures of the Democratic Republic of America, no later than January 21 of the year of issuance.

The term of debt and interest on any issuance of debt shall not exceed 10 years, and must be paid in full by the end of the 10th year.

The third barrier to corruption is to eliminate the elite power to increase the supply of money, and to control interest rates that benefit the corrupt tyranny.

The National Congress shall have the power to coin money, regulate the value thereof, regulate the circulation and creation of money and money instruments, regulate the national banking system and establish the currency value of foreign coin, and fix the Standard of Weights and Measures.

The fourth barrier to corruption is to place the banking system and the Federal Reserve System under the control of the House. The House is given an explicit mission to promote economic growth.

The House has the exclusive power to charter and regulate a system of national banks designed to promote interstate and international commerce and maximum rates of economic growth among all Democratic Republic. The House imposes restrictions on the domain of power and authority of the system of national banks, and restricts the domain of the bank's authority to promote the economic welfare of sovereign Democratic Republic and sovereign citizens.

These four provisions in the new constitution work in tandem with the public purpose mission of the Constitution, stated in the Preamble,

We, the citizens of the Democratic Republic of America, establish this constitutional contract between our respective states and the National Government of the Democratic Republic of America.

We solemnly swear and affirm that we establish this contract to preserve and protect the natural and civil rights of citizens in each state, and to protect and defend the sovereignty of each state and the nation, from foreign and domestic threats.

Chapter 8.
Slavery, Racism and Secession.

The cultural values that initially bound the citizens of America together, and compelled voluntary allegiance to the rule of law, are stated in the Declaration of Independence.

Those cultural values revolved around protecting individual natural rights.

Madison had to evade the cultural values of natural rights in order to implement his civil rules of procedure that elevated the financial interests of the natural aristocracy over the interests of common citizens.

Consequently, Madison deliberately left out reference to natural rights, deliberately left out reference to the Articles of Confederation, and left out any reference to the terms of surrender by King George, that designated that he surrendered to 13 independent sovereign states.

In contrast to mutual and reciprocal duties, Madison's Constitution creates a consolidated, centralized authority that is one-sided in its treatment of mutual obligations.

In Madison, the elites make the law, and the common citizens are bound to obey the law created by the elites.

The two social classes, the natural aristocracy and the common class, in Madison, did not share common values at the get-go of his Constitution.

The southern plantation society did not share cultural values of New England bankers and merchants.

Madison waited until the last day of the regular Convention to pull off his strategy of combining the two alien cultures.

His notes for September 12, 1787, contain his acknowledgement of how he implemented his strategy,

September 12.

Committee of Style reported a 7 Article document which was read by paragraph. This document (the Constitution), is preceded by a preamble, which begins, "We the People of the United States, in order to form a more perfect union..." rather than "We the people of the states of New Hampshire, etc..."

The other delegates had never seen this version of the Preamble before, but the fix was in, and without debate, 37 of them voted to ratify the Constitution, on September 15, 1787.

By evading the cultural values of equal rights, Madison's amoral rules spelled out how slaves should be counted for taxation and voting apportionment decisions, without addressing the larger moral issue of slavery.

The morality of slavery was irreconcilably opposed to "All citizens are created equal," which Madison had to evade, in order to bring the slave states into the new government.

Slavery was viewed by Madison as a commercial faction, to be balanced against the commercial faction of shipping and banking.

Madison's attempt to combine the financial faction of slavery with the northern commercial factions failed for a variety of reasons.

The small states were never satisfied that their interests were mutual to the big states.

The southern slave states were never satisfied that their interests in perpetuating slavery were reciprocal to the northern state's interest in trade and commerce.

The bankers and merchants of the north feared and distrusted the political power of the southern planters.

The two cultures, in 1787, shared no common values, just as today, where the socialist Democrats share no common values with natural rights conservatives.

The consequence of Madison's strategy of combining the slaveocracy with New England's cultural values is that the issue of slavery was never resolved.

The politics of slavery led to periodic attempts to dissolve the nation.

On July 9th, 1787, John Dickinson, delegate from Delaware, wrote in his private notebook about the morality of including slavery as a founding principle in Madison's Constitution.

Dickson wrote,

> Acting before the World, What will be said of this new principle of founding a Right to govern Freemen on a power derived from Slaves,... [who are] themselves incapable of governing yet giving to others what they have not. The omitting [of] the WORD will be regarded as an Endevour to conceal a principle of which we are ashamed.

The morality of slavery was intertwined with the ideology of racism that black people were unable to govern themselves.

The broader issue at the Convention was about who was fit to govern in a representative republic.

All of the elites, including Madison, believed that all blacks, and all common citizens, were unfit to govern.

Madison believed that only the natural aristocracy were fit to govern, because they possessed the moral quality of "virtue."

The debate about slavery and racism was couched in terms of civil rules of procedure for voting and apportionment.

From Madison's notes,

Mr. BUTLER and General PINCKNEY insisted that blacks be included in the rule of representation equally with the whites; and for that purpose moved that the words "three-fifths" be struck out.

Mr. GERRY thought that three-fifths of them was, to say the least, the full proportion that could be admitted.

The delegates then proceeded to go around and around the issue of how to count slaves.

From Madison's notes,

It was then moved by Mr. RUTLEDGE, seconded by Mr. BUTLER, to add to the words, "equitable ratio of representation," at the end of the motion just agreed to, the words "according to the quotas of contribution."

Mr. WILSON, seconded by Mr. PINCKNEY, this was postponed; in order to add, after the words, "equitable ratio of representation," the words following: "in proportion to the whole number of white and other free citizens and inhabitants of every age, sex and condition, including those bound to servitude for a term of years, and three-fifths of all other persons not comprehended in the foregoing description, except Indians not paying taxes, in each State" — this being the rule in the act of Congress, agreed to by eleven States, for apportioning quotas of revenue on the States, and requiring a census only every five, seven, or ten years.

Mr. GERRY thought property not the rule of representation. Why, then, should the blacks, who were property in the South, be in the rule of representation more than the cattle and horses of the North?

Mr. GOUVERNEUR MORRIS was compelled to declare himself reduced to the dilemma of doing injustice to the Southern States, or to human nature; and he must therefore do it to the former. For he could never agree to give such encouragement to the slave trade, as would be given by allowing them a representation for their negroes; and he did not believe those States would ever confederate on terms that would deprive them of that trade.

Without constitutional protection of slavery, the southern states would not join the Union.

The issue of slavery then turned to taxation of slaves and the sanction to permit the slave trade. As noted by Rutledge, "the issue of religion and humanity had nothing to do with this question."

From Madison's notes,

August 21.

Mr. L. MARTIN proposed to vary Article 7, Section 4, so as to allow a prohibition or tax on the importation of slaves. In the first place, as five slaves are to be counted as three freemen, in the apportionment of Representatives, such a clause would leave an encouragement to this traffic. In the second place, slaves weakened one part of the Union, which the other parts were bound to protect; the privilege of importing them was therefore unreasonable. And in the third place, it was inconsistent with the principles of the Revolution, and dishonorable to the American character, to have such a feature in the Constitution.

Mr. RUTLEDGE did not see how the importation of slaves could be encouraged by this section. He was not apprehensive of insurrections, and would readily exempt the other States from the obligation to protect the Southern against them. Religion and humanity had nothing to do with this question. Interest alone is the governing principle with nations. The true question at present is, whether the Southern States shall or shall not be parties to the Union. If the Northern States consult their interest, they will not oppose the increase of slaves, which will increase the commodities of which they will become the carriers.

Mr. ELLSWORTH was for leaving the clause as it stands. Let every State import what it pleases. The morality or wisdom of slavery are considerations belonging to the States themselves. What enriches a part enriches the whole, and the States are the best judges of their particular interest. The old Confederation had not meddled with this point; and he did not see any greater necessity for bringing it within the policy of the new one.

August 23.

In Convention, — Governor LIVINGSTON, from the Committee of eleven, to whom were referred the two remaining clauses of the fourth Section, and the fifth and sixth Sections of the seventh Article, delivered in the following Report:

"Strike out so much of the fourth Section as was referred to the Committee, and insert, 'The migration or importation of such persons as the several States, now existing, shall think proper to admit, shall not be prohibited by the Legislature prior to the year 1800; but a tax or duty may be imposed on such migration or importation, at a rate not exceeding the average of the duties laid on imports.'

August 29.

Mr. BUTLER moved to insert after Article 15, "If any person bound to service or labor in any of the United States, shall escape into another State, he or she shall not be discharged from such service or labor, in consequence of any regulations subsisting in the State to which they escape, but shall be delivered up to the person justly claiming their service or labor," — which was agreed to, nem. con.

Delegates from the Southern states were adamant that they would not join the Union if the Constitution prohibited slavery or the slave trade. Their last demand, in August, was that non-slave states return runaway slaves to their owners in slave states.

From Madison's notes,

Mr. PINCKNEY. South Carolina can never receive the plan if it prohibits the slave-trade. In every proposed extension of the powers of Congress, that State has expressly and watchfully excepted that of meddling with the importation of negroes. If the States be all left at liberty on this subject, South Carolina may perhaps, by degrees do of herself what is wished, as Virginia and Maryland already have done.

August 22.

Mr. SHERMAN was for leaving the clause as it stands. He disapproved of the slave-trade; yet as the States were now possessed of the right to import slaves, as the public good did not require it to be taken from them, and as it was expedient to have as few objections as possible to the proposed scheme of government, he thought it best to leave the matter as we find it. He observed that the abolition of slavery seemed to be going on in the United States, and that the good sense of the several States would probably by degrees complete it. He urged on the Convention the necessity of despatching its business.

Mr. PINCKNEY. If slavery be wrong, it is justified by the example of all the world. He cited the case of Greece, Rome, and other ancient states; the sanction given by France, England, Holland, and other modern states. In all ages one half of mankind have been slaves. If the Southern States were let alone, they will probably of themselves stop importations. He would himself, as a citizen of South Carolina, vote for it. An attempt to take away the right, as proposed, will produce serious objections to the Constitution, which he wished to see adopted...He contended, that the importation of slaves would be for the interest of the whole Union. The more slaves, the more produce to employ the carrying trade; the more consumption also; and the more of this, the more revenue for the common treasury. He admitted it to be reasonable that slaves should be dutied like other imports; but should consider a rejection of the clause as an exclusion of South Carolina from the Union.

Mr. RUTLEDGE. If the Convention thinks that North Carolina, South Carolina, and Georgia, will ever agree to the plan, unless their right to import slaves be untouched, the expectation is vain. The people of those States will never be such fools as to give up so important an interest. He was strenuous against striking out the section, and seconded the motion of General PINCKNEY for a commitment.

Mr. WILSON did not well see, on what principle the admission of blacks in the proportion of three-fifths, could be explained. Are they admitted as citizens — then why are they not admitted on an equality with white citizens? Are they admitted as property — then why is not other property admitted into the computation? These were difficulties, however, which he thought must be overruled by the necessity of compromise. He had some apprehensions also, from the tendency of the blending of the blacks with the whites, to give disgust to the people of Pennsylvania, as had been intimated by his colleague (Mr. GOUVERNEUR MORRIS). But he differed from him in thinking numbers of inhabitants so incorrect a measure of wealth. He had seen the western settlements of Pennsylvania, and on a comparison of them with the city of Philadelphia could discover little other difference, than that property was more unequally divided here than there. Taking the same number in the aggregate, in the two situations, he believed there would be little difference in their wealth and ability to contribute to the public wants.

At the very end of the Convention, as he did throughout the Convention, George Mason defended Jefferson's principles of the natural rights republic. He attempted to explain that the commercial and financial forces that promoted slavery were global in scope, and were primarily perpetuated by the upper class of Great Britain.

Colonel MASON.

This infernal traffic originated in the avarice of British merchants. The British Government constantly checked the attempts of Virginia to put a stop to it. The present question concerns not the importing States alone, but the whole Union. The evil of having slaves was experienced during the late war. Had slaves been treated as they might have been by the enemy, they would have proved dangerous instruments in their hands. But their folly dealt by the slaves as it did by the tories. He mentioned the dangerous insurrections of the slaves in Greece and Sicily; and the instructions given by Cromwell to the commissioners sent to Virginia, to arm the servants and slaves, in case other means of obtaining its submission should fail. Maryland and Virginia, he said, had already prohibited the importation of slaves expressly. North Carolina had done the same in substance. All this would be in vain, if South Carolina and Georgia be at liberty to import.

Just prior to the vote to approve Madison's Constitution, on September 15, 1787, the 37 delegates tightened up the language and sanctions against free states that did not return slaves to their owners.

There was no discussion and no debate about the fugitive slave clause, before the final vote was taken.

From Madison's notes,

September 15.

Took up Article IV, Section 2 (Fugitive Slave clause):

Struck out "no person legally held to service or labor in one state escaping into another" and replaced it with "no person held to service or labor in one state, under the laws thereof, escaping into another.

The issue of slavery was the key issue in the debates over Madison's Constitution, and the Black Democrat activists today are correct that Madison's Constitution was conceived under the sin of slavery.

Jefferson's Declaration, and the Articles of Confederation, were not conceived under the sin of slavery.

Madison's Constitution did not prohibit secession, and because the Constitution did not state the moral principles that bound different factions together, the various factions felt entitled to leave the Union, when political decisions did not favor their interests.

In addition to evading the issue of slavery, Madison could not implement his plan, unless it contained "We, the people, and not the states. Madison supported the philosophy expressed by George Read, that "We, the people," replaced the states.

From Madison's notes,

Mr. READ disliked the idea of guaranteeing territory. It abetted the idea of distinct States, which would be a perpetual source of discord. There can be no cure for this evil but in doing away States altogether, and uniting them all into one great society.

Read liked his idea about eliminating the states so much that on September 17, 1787, he signed the document twice. Of the 37 signatures, Read signed once for himself and once for John Dickinson, who was home sick with a migraine.

As a historical fact, only 36 delegates actually signed the Constitution because Read, without legal authority, signed twice.

In other words, of the 75 original delegates to the Convention, less than 50% actually signed the document.

Most of the threats to secede were about the unresolved issue of slavery, and the underlying philosophy of racism.

Up until 1861, most of the threats to leave were political posturing to extract concessions from the other factions.

Some of the early threats to leave were about the financial interests of the natural aristocracy, who had organized themselves into a political party called the Federalists.

The issue of slavery and secession were left unresolved by Madison, even though Madison used the ploy that states had a fundamental right to leave the Union during the ratification debates.

Madison had no choice about slavery because the Southern delegates to the Convention of 1787 had made clear that they would not join the Union without slavery.

From Madison's notes,

Mr. RUTLEDGE. If the Convention thinks that North Carolina, South Carolina, and Georgia, will ever agree to the plan, unless their right to import slaves be untouched, the expectation is vain. The people of those States will never be such fools as to give up so important an interest. He was strenuous against striking out the section, and seconded the motion of General PINCKNEY for a commitment.

August 29.

Mr. GORHAM. If the Government is to be so fettered as to be unable to relieve the Eastern States, what motive can they have to join in it, and thereby tie their own hands from measures which they could otherwise take for themselves? The Eastern States were not led to strengthen the Union by fear for their own safety. He deprecated the consequences of disunion; but if it should take place, it was the Southern part of the continent that had most reason to dread them. He urged the improbability of a combination against the interest of the Southern States, the different situations of the Northern and Middle States being a security against it. It was, moreover, certain, that foreign ships would never be altogether excluded, especially those of nations in treaty with us.

Mr. SHERMAN proposed, that the proportion of suffrage in the first branch should be according to the respective numbers of free inhabitants; and that in the second branch, or Senate, each State should have one vote and no more. He said, as the States would remain possessed of certain individual rights, each State ought to be able to protect itself; otherwise, a few large States will rule the rest. The House of Lords in England, he observed, had certain particular rights under the Constitution, and hence they have an equal vote with the House of Commons, that they may be able to defend their rights.

Mr. FRANKLIN "I must own, that I was originally of opinion it would be better if every member of Congress, or our national Council, were to consider himself rather as a representative of the whole, than as an agent for the interests of a particular State; in which case the proportion of members for each State would be of less consequence, and it would not be very material whether they voted by States or individually. But as I find this is not to be expected, I now think the number of representatives should bear some proportion to the number of the represented; and that the decisions should be by the majority of members, not by the majority of the States.

On Mr. BUTLER'S motion, for considering blacks as equal to whites in the apportionment of representation, — Delaware, South Carolina, Georgia, aye — 3; Massachusetts, Connecticut, New Jersey, Pennsylvania, Maryland, Virginia, North Carolina, no — 7; New York, not on the floor.

In order to hide their endorsement of slavery, the delegates, at the very last moment, modified the clause on the guarantee of a Republican form of government.

From Madison's notes,

Alterations having been made in the Resolution, making it read, "that a Republican constitution, and its existing laws, ought to be guaranteed to each State by the United States," the whole was agreed to, nem. con.

George Nicholas, a Federalist ally of Madison, stated during the time of the convention in Philadelphia, and again later, in the Virginia ratifying convention, that if "the Federal Government abused its powers, Virginia could withdraw from the union."

Madison knew, at the time Nicholas made this statement, that it was false.

During the Virginia Legislature's ratification debate, Madison chose not to correct this statement made by Nicholas, on the floor.

By leaving unchallenged the subterfuge of secession related to slavery, Madison's flawed Constitution provoked the Civil War.

The Southern states assumed that they had a legal right to secede.

During the debate over the 1798 Sedition Act, Madison again wrote that states had a right to nullify Federal legislation and to secede.

Southern states assumed that the Father of the Constitution was the ultimate voice of authority on the issue of secession.

Their vote to leave in 1861 was predicated on this belief.

After Jefferson won the election, in 1801, the Federalists were afraid that his government would upset their unequal rights and privileges.

In March of 1801, the Federalists refused to inaugurate Jefferson, and the Governor of Virginia called out the militia to prepare for war with the Federalists.

As early as 1804, Timothy Pickering of Massachusetts and a few other Federalists, envisioned creating a separate New England confederation, possibly combining with lower Canada to form a new pro-British nation.

The Embargo Act of 1807 was seen by the New England aristocracy as a threat promoted by Jefferson to the economy of Massachusetts, and the state legislature debated in May, 1808, how the state should respond.

In 1809, the legislature of Massachusetts issued an ultimatum to the Federal government on the Embargo Act. The ultimatum stated that the Embargo Act was intolerable, and that the state would be forced to leave the Union.

The negative effects of the embargo were primarily on bankers and merchants, perpetuating the social class conflict inherent in Madison's Constitution.

The embargo negatively affected the levels of bank loans, the bank-issued component of the money supply. The values of financial stock and bond yields fell, directly affecting the financial welfare of the wealthy elites, who owned the stocks and bonds.

The positive economic effects of the embargo on the rest of the nation, outside of New England, was a dramatic increase in domestic manufacturing and a strengthening of the domestic income multiplier effects, primarily in small manufacturing supply chains.

Fighting the embargo by New England elites was a precursor to the first significant threat to secede.

According to the Federalists, the War of 1812, negatively affected their financial interests in shipping and trade with Great Britain.

The Federalists claimed that the War was primarily about protecting the interests of the southern slaveocracy. The Federalists deployed a subterfuge that their opposition to the War was primarily about political domination by the "Virginia dynasty."

In 1813, the Legislature of Massachusetts called for a convention of New England states to secede.

The Hartford Convention of 1814 convened the secret meeting of Federalists, many of whom had signed, or supported the enactment of Madison's Constitution. The Federalists continued to work out the plan to secede by extending the earlier plan of Pickering to form a new pro-British nation.

During the New England debate on secession, no political faction, in either the Federal government, or the other states, objected to the idea that the states had a right to secede.

The southern states assumed that the northern states had a right to secede.

After 1814, the issue of slavery continued to roil the political factions, with various states threatening to leave if the western states were admitted to the Union as slave states.

Henry Clay, of Kentucky, was able to avert secession with his Missouri Compromise of 1820. The Missouri Compromise was successful in delaying the threats of secession until the late 1830's, with the election of Andrew Jackson.

Jackson's populist appeal to common citizens again served to threaten the financial interests of New England elites. The issue of slavery was the political subterfuge that the elites used to attack Jackson's animosity to the Second Bank.

In the early 1830s, the issue of trade and tariffs again erupted between northern and southern states. This time, the debate was both about secession and nullification.

In 1832, the South Carolina Exposition and Protest stated in a resolution that, "Levying tariffs for the purpose of promoting New England manufacturing was not an enumerated power."

The resolution stated that the "Compact was between the sovereign states and the federal government."

The Constitution, according to South Carolina, was created by 13 concurrent state majorities, and the states retained a negative on the acts of the majority.

In 1832 the South Carolina legislature passed the Ordinance of Nullification, which stated that if the federal government used military force to enforce the tariff, South Carolina would secede.

In response Daniel Webster switched sides from his earlier advocacy of northern secession and stated that the Constitution was the creation of the whole people, "We, the people," and not individual states.

The southern states, therefore, according to Webster, did not have a right to nullify the Acts of Congress because the states were not parties to the contract.

In the early 1840s, New England abolitionists began meeting to plan how the non-slave states could secede.

In 1843, the Massachusetts Anti-Slavery Society endorsed secession of the northern states, by a vote of 59 to 21.

Throughout the 1840s to the election of Lincoln, in 1859, the issue of slavery continued to animate political conflict in the Nation. As they did during the Convention of 1787, the Slaveocracy threatened to leave if they did not get their way on slavery, the slave trade, or fugitive slaves.

In 1856, Governor Henry Wise, of Virginia, issued a plea to other southern governors to meet to plot secession. Their main fear was that if the new Republican Party, and the older Whig Party combined to win the election, the southern states would secede.

The slave trade in New York was lucrative because the New York merchants and traders made money by shipping slaves to the South.

In 1861, Fernando Wood, the mayor of New York City, proposed that the city secede from New York State and become its own nation city state, to protect their financial interests in the slave trade.

Lincoln won the election and the first state to secede was Mississippi in December, 1860. It was followed by five more in January, 1861, and Texas on February 1, bringing the total to seven.

These seven states met in Montgomery and formed the Confederate States of America.

In May, 1861, after having first rejected the referendum to secede, North Carolina voted to join the CSA, and the capital was moved from Montgomery to Richmond.

During the Civil War, the western part of Virginia seceded from the state and became West Virginia in 1863. The proximate cause of the secession of West Virginia was slavery.

The secession of West Virginia was unconstitutional because Madison's Constitution, while founded on the principle of

"We, the people," and not on the sovereignty of the individual states, none-the-less required that no part of a state could secede without the approval of the other states.

Partial secession, in other words, was prohibited by Madison, but full state secession of the Southern states was not prohibited, until 1869.

Texas v. White, (1869), was a case argued before the United States Supreme Court in 1869. The case involved a claim by the Republican Reconstruction Government of Texas that the United States bonds owned by the State of Texas had been illegally sold by the Confederate state government, during the Civil War.

The Supreme Court followed the legal reasoning of Lincoln that the Southern states never really seceded. Lincoln maintained that there was no Confederate States of America, and that the 13 southern states were in rebellion, not war.

The Supreme Court ruled that Texas had remained a United States state ever since it first joined the Union, despite its joining the Confederate States of America.

While there is no text in the Constitution about secession, the court further held that the Constitution contained a penumbra that did not permit states to unilaterally secede from the United States.

The Court further ruled that the ordinances of secession, and all the acts of the legal acts of seceding states intended to give effect to such ordinances, were "absolutely null".

From 1869 to today, the act of secession of a state is prohibited by a decision of the Supreme Court, not by the Constitution.

Madison's ambiguity and inconsistency in the Constitution has led the Nation into an unsolvable quagmire around the legacy of slavery, and the underlying ideology of racism that black people are unfit to govern.

Either "All people are created equal," or, they are born into the shackles of slavery, never to escape bondage.

Either the 10th Amendment is valid, or the centralized government has unlimited, implied powers.

Either the nation is "We, the people," or 13 independent states. Depending on the circumstances, Madison fluctuated on the question.

Either states have a right to secede, or they don't. Madison played both sides of the issue.

The southern states either left the nation to form the CSA, or they did not.

The 14th Amendment was either ratified by the states in a legitimate ratification process, or the ratification of the Amendment was a fraud.

The North's victory in the Civil War did not solve any of Madison's inconsistencies. The primary difference now is that the issue of slavery and racism has been adopted by the socialist Democrats to promote their ideology of global socialism.

As explained by Merrill Jensen, in his book, Articles of Confederation, what the anti-federalist did not understand, in 1781, was that the degree of ideological commitment of the elites to creating a government that protected their privileges.

Jensen writes,

> …the nationalists adopted a theory of the sovereignty of the people, in the name of the people, and erected a nationalistic government whose purpose was to thwart the will of the people in whose name they acted…

In turn, Jensen explains that what Madison failed to see, in 1787, was that the one-sided government that he had created would be captured in 2008, by elected leaders who were traitors to the sovereign interests of the nation.

Madison did not anticipate that elected representatives would hate the Nation that they governed.

This is exactly the outcome that George Mason predicted, when he said that Madison's Constitution would end in an aristocratic tyranny.

Except that Mason did not anticipate that it would be a socialist elite tyranny that captured the central government.

The use of the rhetoric of hate by the Democrats, today, creates a social climate of violence. The climate of violence will eventually create a civil war, unless the natural rights conservatives adopt a strategy for ending the violence.

The socialists intend to create violence because the chaos and turmoil facilitates their transformation of America into a global socialist state.

According to the strategy of Marx and Lenin, in order to overthrow the capitalist system, the capitalist class must be killed in a violent revolution that "sanctifies" the new socialist state.

The intent of the socialist Democrats is to precipitate violence to overthrow the constitutionally-elected government of President Trump.

The first stages of the violent overthrow is the Democrat's use of intimidation of conservatives in public venues. The use of their violent foot soldiers in Anti-Fa is a ratchet up from intimidation.

As an example of the Democrat's use of hate, in Obama's last year in office, 140 police were slaughtered in America, under Obama's approving gaze.

The killing of police is consistent with the rhetoric of violence used by Democrats to heighten the sense of grievance by oppressed Democrat voters that cops prey upon black people.

Another example is the beating and torture on FaceBook by the four blacks in Chicago on the disabled white victim. Those four black people stated, during their video, that they hate all white people.

The continual invocation of the rhetoric of hate was used by Obama to condition those four blacks to perpetrate violence against white people.

Those four black people are representative of all Democrats.They will indiscriminately kill white people, simply and solely, because the Democrats conditioned them to hate all white people.

Obama, and the Democrats, are able to turn on and off the violence, whenever Soros tells them to. This pattern of violence is a very effective tool of social control because the violence creates the conditions of civil chaos that socialists require to implement their revolution.

The only viable, non-violent, strategy for dealing with the Democrats is to facilitate voluntary dissolution of the Nation.

Democrat socialists have a natural right to renounce their citizenship, and move to the new Socialist States of America.

In a flip-flop of history from Justice Marshall's decision in Marbury, on the issue of "We, the people," Justice Kennedy, in 1995, said,

"Our federalism requires that Congress treat the states in a manner consistent with their status as residuary sovereigns and joint participants in the governance of the nation."

This type of judicial flip-flopping is a common feature of American judicial history because there cannot be a strict interpretation of the text of the Constitution.

The interpretation of the text depends on the ideological predisposition of the Justices who serve at that moment in history.

If the Southern states had been sovereign, as Justice Kennedy stated, then Lincoln's Civil War would not have been constitutional.

But, Lincoln believed that the nation was created by "We, the people," and therefore, Lincoln felt justified in saving the "Union," at any cost.

Lincoln's War solved nothing in Madison's flawed document. The underlying flaws in Madison's Constitution remain, and are not resolvable by amending or modifying the text.

The text unleashed an enduring saga of racism, based upon Madison's implicit endorsement of slavery.

After the Civil War, the former Plantation Aristocracy formed the Democrat "Party of Our Fathers," on the idealized version of history that the Civil War had been a grand effort to protect the "Southern Way of Life."

The loss of the southern states to the northern states was reinterpreted by the Plantation elite as the "Lost Cause."

The Lost Cause, in their minds, meant the loss of elite domination over black people. They formed the Ku Klux Klan, and implemented apartheid in the South, based upon their racist version of slavery and black people.

The "Party of Our Fathers" combined racism against blacks with an appeal to white supremacy of common whites that proved irresistible.

Towards the end of Federal occupation, (1875), according to Otto Olsen, in Reconstruction and Redemption in the South, the Bourbon Democrats regained their political footing, and made it clear that they "...sought to destroy rather than compete with Republicanism, and that they were willing to utilize any means necessary to do so..."

It took the Democrats about 25 years to make good on their promise to destroy the nascent Republican Populist political movement.

The Democrats undermined the Republican Populist Party by infiltrating the farmer's organizations and subverting the political allegiance of the farmers, based upon appeals to white supremacy.

A leader of the Democratic Party, in an 1874 letter to the Greensboro Patriot, said "We assure the Negro equality before the law, but we also assure that we will strike down the Republican Party forever."

In a letter of 1891, Robert Rhett wrote to North Carolina State Representative Joseph Wheeler, a Democrat and laid out the strategy for destruction of the Republican Party,

> I deem it of the utmost importance, that strong and substantial Democrats throughout this District should enter the order and control it, as they readily can do, if they choose and will go to the trouble.

The political collaboration between white farmers and Black Republicans was called fusion, and it was a drastic threat to the progeny of the Plantation.

"At issue," for the populists, according to Bruce Palmer, in Man Over Money, was not private ownership of wealth and property but their concentration in a few hands. A wider distribution of private property through equalization of opportunities would correct this.

The same interpretation of the Populism is given by Carl Degler, in The Other South, who wrote,

> The Agrarians did not object to the (free market) system; they merely wanted a fair chance to prosper under it. They had been led to believe...that America was the home of opportunity.

As a part of their political reforms in North Carolina, in 1892, the Republicans attempted to use property taxes to educate black children.

The use of tax dollars to educate black children provided the needed propaganda for the Democrats to tar the farmers and Republicans with the epithet that the Republicans loved Negroes, better than they loved white people.

Eventually, it was the threat posed by the political coalition of common whites and blacks, in the guise of the Republican Populist Party, that led to the violent counter-attack of the Bourbon Democrats, using the war cry of "Negro Rule."

Beginning in 1898, the war cry of "Negro Rule" was successful in banishing the Republican Party from Southern states for at least 100 years.

According to Paul Escott, the

> Elite Democrats did more than beat back the challenge of the Agrarians, disfranchise black people, and stigmatize cooperation between Tar Heels of both races. They imposed an undemocratic electoral system, so complete and effective that all future political discourse had a restricted character.

The Democrats were successful, in November of 1898, in conducting the nation's first military coup d'etate to overthrow a constitutionally elected Wilmington city government of black city councillors.

According to press reports of the coup, the Cape Fear River was swollen with the carcasses of unarmed blacks who had been killed by the Democrats.

The Democrats chortled their victory in a telegram from the Democrat military leaders in Wilmington to the Democrat political leaders in Raleigh. The telegram read,

"We have taken the city."

According to Escott, after the coup of 1898, Democratic Party leaders were quoted as saying that,

> we will no longer be ruled, and we will never be ruled by men of African origin.

Furnifold Simmons, Chairman of the State Democratic Party, and a long time U. S. Senator from North Carolina said in 1898,

> North Carolina is a White Man's State, and White Men will rule it, and they will crush the party of Negro domination beneath a majority so overwhelming that no other party will ever dare to establish Negro rule here.

In seeking to justify the coup, the Wilmington Semi-Weekly Messenger wrote:

> Intelligent citizens...owning the greatest percent of the property and paying the greatest percent of the taxes should rule.

Furnifold Simmons solicited contributions from "...the bankers, railroad executives, lawyers and manufacturing interests, and promised that the Democrats would not raise corporation taxes if the Democrats regained power."

The alliance the Democrats sought was between the white racist party and the corporate elite. This is the same coalition, today between global socialists and global corporations, which rules the swamp.

The political contract between racist Democrats and the corporate elite was based upon racism.

In exchange for corporate support of one-party white apartheid rule in North Carolina, the Democrats promised the corporate elite not to raise corporate taxes, preferring always to shift the burden to common citizens through the use of sales and property taxes.

The violence of the Democrats in North Carolina, beginning in 1900, included the forced sterilization of black people who were considered by the Democrats to be too insane to have children.

The official state-sanctioned language used by the Democrats for the sterilization program was black insanity.

The common phrase used by the Democrats for insane black people was "uppity" blacks who had voted with the white Republicans. Their insanity was demonstrated by their coalition with Republicans.

The forced sterilization of black people by the government of North Carolina finally ended in the mid-1970s.

By that time, 50,000 black people, both males and females, had been sterilized.

As a political strategy, the forced sterilization of uppity blacks was a huge political success for the Democrats.

With the DNA genetics of uppity Blacks purged from society, Blacks in North Carolina now vote almost 100% for the Democrats.

Much of the violence of the Plantation elite took place under the auspices of the Klan, whose leadership mirrored the leadership of the Democratic Party.

During the day, the prominent Democrats held elected offices and wielded official power. At night, they donned their robes and hoods, and went out looking for uppity blacks to lynch.

The contract between the Democrats and the corporate elite was held together by the constant threat that Negroes would be used to replace white workers in the textile mills.

The Democrats made the threat, which was implemented by the textile, tobacco and furniture elite, an effective economic use of racism derived from a position of Democratic Party political monopoly.

The lesson that common white factory workers learned from this system was that if they ever voted for Republicans or Populist Agrarians again, they would lose their jobs.

In his analysis of how the Bourbon Democrats destroyed the Republican Party, V. O. Key noted that the system of apartheid imposed on the South was not simply about "white supremacy."

He said,

> the issue of Negro suffrage is a question not of white supremacy but the supremacy of which whites.

The philosophy that undergird the Democratic assault combined their view that Blacks were an inferior race with the view that common whites were unfit to govern.

The philosophical hostility towards political rights for certain individuals originated in the unresolved differences between the values about individual freedom, contained in the Declaration of Independence, and the absence of those moral values in Madison's constitutional rules.

Writing in 1922, in The Journal of Social Forces, Ashby Jones connected the paternalistic collectivism of the plantation elites to the cultural collectivism that viewed all blacks as a social class.

> Although upper-class whites had inherited a benevolent feeling toward the individual Negro, they expressed a social and political fear of the race en masse. This dehumanization of blacks among the better classses of southern whites was responsible for the unspeakable record of barbaritees committed against this weaker race.

In adopting race hatred as a political weapon to promote socialism, Obama deployed the rhetorical charade that the Democrats were not the party of racism.

Obama said,

> There's not a black America and white America," at the 2004, Democrat Convention, "there's the United States of America.

As explained by Noam Scheiber in his May 30, 2004, New Republic article:

> Whereas many working-class voters are wary of African American candidates, whom they think will promote black interests at the expense of their own, they simply don't see Obama in these terms. This allows him to appeal to white voters on traditional Democratic issues like jobs, health care, and education—just like a white candidate would.

After Obama was elected, he continued using the rhetoric and imagery of slavery because it is such a useful tool for making black Americans hate America.

Obama's strategy was to keep the grievances of slavery vivid. The image of slavery at the founding of the Constitution of 1787 will never end, as a political tool, for the socialist Democrats.

As Obama said, in March 2008, Madison's constitution was irrevocably flawed:

> The document they produced was eventually signed but ultimately unfinished. It was stained by this nation's original sin of slavery, a question that divided the colonies and brought the convention to a stalemate until the founders chose to allow the slave trade to continue for at least twenty more years, and to leave any final resolution to future generations.

Throughout his tenure, Obama continually invoked the symbols of racism and slavery, in a three step political strategy, to transform America into a global socialist state.

The first part of his strategy was to create race hatred between socialists and non-socialists, in order to attract converts who began to hate America, and who had a heightened sense of grievance about the founding of the Nation.

The second part of Obama's strategy was to promise the aggrieved and downtrodden citizens that he and the Democrats, would remedy their grievances against the right-wing forces that were oppressing them.

The final part of Obama's strategy was to use tax-funded welfare payments to hook the downtrodden into a life of dependency on the socialist government.

Obama understood that once the citizens become servile to the State, they would lose their capacity for rational decision-making, the bedrock citizen requirement in a natural rights republic.

Lyndon Johnson, Democrat President, made this same connection between welfare payments and Democrat political dominance. After passing the first phase of his Great Society welfare program, in 1963, Johnson stated,

> These Negroes, they're getting pretty uppity these days and that's a problem for us since they've got something now they never had before, the political pull to back up their uppityness. Now we've got to do something about this, we've got to give them a little something, just enough to quiet them down, not enough to make a difference... I'll have them niggers voting Democratic for the next two hundred years.

Obama knew that his hardest job in his conversion process was the very first part of making citizens hate America.

Given the image of NFL players kneeling during the National Anthem, for no objective reason, it is clear that Obama was successful in his use of race hatred.

At the same 2004 Democrat convention where Obama spoke, the black nationalist, Al Sharpton, complained that Lincoln had promised the slaves that they would get "40 acres and a mule."

According to Sharpton, the Republicans never made good on their promise, and according to Democrats, the Republicans will never make good on their promise because Republicans are fundamentally, and forever, racists.

In his last weeks of office, Obama continually invoked the legacy of racism and slavery to heighten the fear of Democrats of President Trump.

"We have, by no means overcome the legacies of slavery and Jim Crow and colonialism and racism," he said.

As he did with using the agency of the IRS to undermine the rule of law, Obama unleashed the deep state spy apparatus to find some pretext for halting Trump's inauguration.

The central tenant of the Democrat socialist religion is that the minority of socialist elites are much smarter than the citizens, and therefore, the socialist elites should have all the constitutional power to make decisions.

The socialist Democrats have learned that the cultural values of "We, the people," collectivism, was an effective weapon for controlling both blacks and whites, who are seen by the Democrat socialists as collectivist identity groups "not fit" to participate in political decisions.

Once the Democrats were successful in having both blacks and common whites view the Republicans as a collectivist group, to be vilified and hated, their political system became much more effective at maintaining political power.

If the socialists are successful in taking over the central government, there is nothing in Madison's Constitution stopping them from permanently imposing their special form of slavery on the non-socialists.

They will take over the institutional mechanisms of power designed by Madison for the natural elite.

The historical consequence of Madison's flawed arrangement is neither a representative republic, based upon the rule of law, nor a system of government, based on the natural rights of the consent of the governed.

Madison's government ended in a centralized global tyranny, operated for the benefit of the few global elites, against the many.

In the case of Democrat socialist subjugation, or slavery, the socialist political elite hold institutional structural power, derived from Madison's rules, not from the consent of the governed.

Rather than the voluntary allegiance to the rule of law, the structural power grants undelegated authority to socialist elites to compel, against a citizen's sovereign will, obedience to the socialist state.

The structural power denies the individual citizen the freedom to break away from the subjugation. In this instance, the sovereign life mission of the common citizen is subjugated to the greater glory of social welfare of the State.

This institutional structural power is the operative force in Madison's Constitution that elevates the financial interests of the elites over the class interests of common citizens.

His "balance of power," and 3 branches of "checks and balances," is the framework of constitutional structural power that can not be altered or abolished.

His arrangement bestows undelegated, unelected power to the elites in the swamp.

In Madison's Constitution, both the individual states, and the individual citizen's freedom to leave the constitutional relationship, without resort to violence, is nonexistent.

Madison's Constitution can possibly continue for states that choose not to leave the United States of America, if and when, the socialists leave to form their Socialist States of America.

A better solution to re-store the natural rights republic is to start over with a new nation, under the new Constitution of the Democratic Republic of America, which reconnects the nation to the principles stated in the Declaration of Independence.

In order to correct Madison's flawed document, and his enduring legacy of racism, the Constitution of the Democratic Republic of America contains the following components:

From the principles of government:

"...that individual citizens who freely give their consent to form a government through constitutional conventions are bound by the original contract until the operation of the government becomes destructive to the original intent of obtaining individual freedom and the pursuit of happiness..."

"...that the parties to the constitutional contract are individual citizens acting through their elected representatives at the state and national levels of government..."

"...that the citizens of each state have mechanisms in place in the constitutional contract to modify or abolish the governments that they have created which have become destructive to the ideals and goals under which the National Government is instituted, including the right of each state to vote on remaining a member of the national government in a referendum to be held every 20 years from the date of admittance..."

"...that the National Government that is created by this union of states shall never usurp the sovereign power or authority of the individual states or the sovereignty of the citizens in each state and that states have an inalienable right to call a convention of the states, without Congressional approval, to modify, amend, or abolish this Constitutional Contract."

"...that the 1776 American Revolution was ordained by God to allow citizens to pursue individual human freedoms and liberty from oppression and is an exceptional model in human history..."

"...that all citizens are created by God with equal natural rights, and that the purpose of the Nation is to protect the equal application of the law to all citizens, regardless of race or religious beliefs…"

From the Bill of Rights:

The right of citizens of the Democratic Republic America to vote, hold elected office, or deliberate in public debates, shall not be denied or abridged by the National Government, or by any State, on account of race, color of skin, sex, or religious beliefs.

From the President's Duties:

It is the constitutional duty of the President to preserve, protect and defend the natural and civil rights of citizens and to defend the sovereign borders of the nation from foreign and domestic threats.

From the Right of Secession and Emigration:

Any state may secede from this Union by a petition ratified by a majority of the state legislature, presented to the National Senate.

The Senate must act upon the petition to grant secession within 14 days.

The grant of secession is irrevocable and permanent.

Notwithstanding the permanency of secession of a state, verified citizens of a partial geographical territory of the former state may petition the Senate for admission as a new state.

A citizen of the Democratic Republic of America may emigrate to a non-member territory or state by a petition of citizenship revocation. A citizen revocation of citizenship is irrevocable and permanent.

The new constitution ends slavery and racism by substituting free market competition for aristocratic financial privilege. Race hatred and race envy ends when all citizens share an equal opportunity for upward occupational mobility.

Individual freedom provides the framework for the free competitive markets to function. In the chronology of events leading to the formation of a natural rights republic, God grants citizens freedom.

From God's grant of freedom, citizens form governments to protect their freedoms.

One of their God-given freedoms is property. Property, protected by government comes first, and then after the protection of property, come free markets, which create the greatest individual and national wealth.

Free markets and free citizens depend on the rule of law to function as a part of a free society.

In a natural rights republic, it is individual freedom that allows entrepreneurs to make money in the future time period from the risky investments that they make in the current time period. Part of this idea is based in Jefferson's notion that citizens own their own labor, and have a natural right to use their labor to create their own happiness.

Without investments, there is no economic growth. Without economic growth, there is no job growth. Without job growth, there is no upward occupational mobility. Without upward occupational mobility in a natural rights republic, common citizens turn to socialism.

Sean Willenz, in The Rise of American Democracy, opens up his study by addressing the absence of the "res publica" or the public thing to be pursued by Madison's conception of the constitution.

The absence of the res publica raises, for Willenz, the overriding question of democracy in America:

> Should unelected private interests, well-connected to government, be permitted to control, for their own benefit, the economic destiny of the entire nation?

According to Willenz, under the set of constitutional rules promoted by Hamilton,

> the idea that the private banking and business community should have special powers in deciding economic policy" was adopted. Without those special powers, according to Hamilton, the wealthy citizens would not have allegiance to the new nation, and without their allegiance, his concept of the free market system would not function well.

In contrast to Hamilton and Madison, the glue that holds the natural rights society together is a common trust in the truth of Jefferson's natural rights.

As Michael Zuckert explains, in The Natural Rights Republic,

> ...the evidentness of the truth is contained within the truths themselves...the truths are not affirmed to be in themselves self-evident, only to be held as such by the Americans...the truths are held as if self evident within the political community dedicated to making them effective. The truths serve as the bedrock or first principles of all political reasoning of the natural rights regime.

Without these common moral values, in the natural rights republic, no force binds citizens to voluntary allegiance to the nation.

The public purpose in the natural rights republic is served by constitutional rules that promote common external values of trust, fair dealing, truthful representations, and promise keeping.

Racism is ended due to cooperation between individuals that occurs when the individuals assume, prior to entering into the exchange process, that these common values are influencing the interpretation of truth the same way, in both citizens to an exchange.

In the natural rights individualist society, the moral freedom of the individual involves the decreasing reliance on externally imposed standards of behavior and ethical values regarding the treatment of others in civil exchanges.

Moral development of the individual occurs during life through an increasing reliance on internalized mental values that address the welfare of others.

The outcome of fair income distribution occurs as a result of the moral values at the beginning of the constitutional exchange, not after the exchange has occurred.

Fairness in the distribution of wealth and income ends racism.

Madison's flaw was his deliberate omission that the ultimate goal of the constitution was protecting individual freedoms.

The Constitution of the Democratic Republic of America corrects Madison's flawed document.

Chapter 9.
Crossing the Rubicon to Create the Democratic Republic of America.

The Roman Republic was based upon allegiance of citizens to obey the unwritten rule of law. The allegiance to the rule of law was voluntary.

The allegiance was sustained because Roman citizens shared widespread cultural values of personal honor that compelled voluntary allegiance to obey the rule of law.

The traditional values that Roman citizens shared were virtue, individual dignity, self-discipline, and sense of duty.

The fall of the Roman Republic was caused by a widespread moral decay of the traditional Roman social and moral codes of behavior, both in the elites and the common citizens.

Cicero explained the fall of the Roman by saying,

> Everybody demands as much political power as he has force behind him. Reason, moderation, law, tradition, duty count for nothing.

In other words, the Roman Republic was based upon respect for the unwritten rule of law that compelled obedience to the written law.

When the respect for the unwritten rule of law eroded, the Roman Republic ended.

When Caesar reached the Rubicon, from his conquest of Gaul, he was aware that respect for rule of law was ending because he had become a victim of the corruption of the Roman Senate.

Before he crossed the Rubicon, he invited a number of Roman historians and philosophers to come to the Rubicon and describe the situation in Rome.

They described the rampant corruption of the Senators, who were using the government to enrich themselves.

After his discussions with the historians, he reached his own psychological Rubicon that the Roman Republic was over.

Part of his motivation to cross the Rubicon was to end the corrupt Roman Republic.

In crossing the Rubicon, Caesar precipitated a 6 year civil war with Pompey, the leader of the corrupt regime in the Roman Senate.

Like the Roman Republic, the American representative republic has ended for the same reasons the Roman Republic ended.

Like the Roman Republic, the American government has been captured by a centralized elite tyranny that uses the agencies of government to enrich themselves.

American natural rights conservatives must cross their own psychological Rubicon that Madison's representative republic did not prevent a corrupt, centralized tyranny.

There are three components to the argument of conservatives crossing the Rubicon:

> 1. The socialists do not share cultural values with conservatives and seek to impose their totalitarian ideology on 63 million Trump voters.
> 2. Madison's Constitution is perfectly suited to imposing the slavery of socialism, based upon Madison's principles of social class elitism.
> 3. The only non-violent solution is to allow the socialists to form their own nation, so that natural

rights conservatives can form the Democratic Republic of America.

Madison's Constitution is no help to citizens in eliminating the tyranny, because Madison's institutional rules of the Constitution serve to protect the elite privileges.

Conservatives must cross the American Rubicon, and conclude that there is nothing of value left in preserving Madison's constitution, or amending it.

In the natural rights republic, citizens have faith that integrity, trust, and the rule of law defines the behavior of all citizens.

American conservative citizens extend to each other a trust that all citizens will obey the law. The conservative's acceptance of his personal allegiance to obey the voluntary self-guiding behavior is the glue that holds the culture and society together.

These moral values were the glue that held the Roman Republic together.

Conservatives continue to make a fundamental, fatal, assumption when they apply their own belief in the rule of law to socialists.

Natural rights conservatives must confront the reality that socialists hate America, and hate the conservative citizens who voted for Trump.

The socialists will never voluntarily obey the unwritten American rule of law because they will never share the cultural belief that all persons, institutions, and entities are subject to the equal application of the law.

Amending the Constitution will not change the behavior of the socialists, or dislodge the corrupt tyranny in the Capital.

Like the Roman Senators, both the corporate and socialist elites in Washington have a profound disrespect for the rule of law.

Attempting to "fix" Madison's Constitution with amendments does nothing to restore respect for the rule of law.

In Jefferson and Locke, the rule of law is like a contract that states that, in return for the benefits of social order, the citizens agree to voluntarily abide by laws and rules.

The equal application of the law to all citizens means that citizens can expect predictable results in justice, no matter the skin color or the wealth.

Predictable results mean that people who act in the same way can expect the law to treat them in the same way.

Socialism is not a commercial or financial faction, as described by Madison.

Socialism does not fit into Madison's Constitution because it is a unified philosophical view of the world. As the socialists use the term in their propaganda, their ideology is aimed at achieving a future state of "social justice."

In Obama's conception of government, the apparatus of government is an instrument of social and political control, used to extract the profits from the capitalist class, in order to give the income to the exploited groups.

Obama seeks to replace the government structure of individual liberty, based upon the Res Publica of the consent of the governed in a representative republic, with the Res Publica of an anti-Americanism socialism.

Socialists in America cannot claim to be Americans, at the same time that they are traitors to America, attempting to assassinate their political enemies.

Democrats cannot, at same time, hate America, and wish the destruction of the nation, while claiming to be Americans.

The Democrat socialists masquerade as Americans because they need the basic liberties of the nation, in order to destroy the nation.

In crossing their own mental Rubicon, American conservatives must reach the conclusion that there are only two options open for dealing with the socialist traitors.

Either the nation can embark on a civil dissolution, where the socialists form their own socialist nation, or the nation can embark on a civil war.

The two cultural value orientations are mutually incompatible and exclusive.

Socialists do not have a moral allegiance to the rule of law, and they have no concept of God-given natural individual rights, because they have no concept of God.

The socialists are ideologically committed to imposing their brand of totalitarian global socialism on the conservatives, but they do not have any moral authority to end the natural rights of a majority of citizens.

The socialists have a natural right to renounce their citizenship, and pursue their new vision, but they have no moral right to impose their vision on the 63 million citizens who want nothing to do with the slavery of government socialism.

The socialists, as predicted by Polybius, are committed to taking over the government by force.

Polybius wrote,

> Once people had grown accustomed to eating off others' tables and expected their daily needs to be met, then, they found someone to champion their cause... they instituted government by force.

The Democrats were successful in corrupting the moral values of a majority of common citizens, who had become accustomed to welfare payments.

Under Democrat socialism, citizens learned that they did not have to take the individual initiative to provide for their own welfare.

Part of the socialist religion begins with the bedrock belief that America is a racist nation that must be destroyed to usher in the era of social justice.

Left-wing ideology is based upon the concepts of skin color, gender, and class privilege.

The socialists believe that certain types of people who are white, and upper class capitalists, are guilty before the fact.

According to critical legal philosophy, all white people must bear the responsibility for acts of oppression committed by their white ancestors.

Left-wing logic is based upon their social construction of reality. Socialists do not believe in absolute truth.

Truth, for socialists, and for socialist critical legal scholars, is relative, and socially-constructed, and is not based upon observable facts.

In the simplified world view of socialism, the two economic classes (capital and labor), exist in perpetuity, and the socialists construct a reality that the economic system of unfair capitalist exchange also exists, as a pre-existing social state of reality.

The socially constructed reality of the term "labor" is expanded to include all the collective identity social groups, identified by the socialist elites, as "disadvantaged" by the operation of the capitalist exchange system.

In socialist ideology, proletariat individuals only exist as a part of their membership in an oppressed collectivist group.

In socialist ideology, a citizen is born into poverty, as a member of a disadvantaged group, and the person is trapped forever, in the social group, like a serf or a slave, by the accident of their birth.

In the multi-cultural socialist application, an individual is born into their group community, and the individual owes her first allegiance and loyalty to that group.

A person is not defined by their own self definition of who they are. They are first, and foremost, an African-American, or a Muslim American, and once identified as a member of a disadvantaged group, they never escape from the identity of that particular "community."

In the socialist Marxist concept of law, all laws are created by elected representatives who are from the capitalist class natural aristocracy, and that the laws that are passed serve those elite financial interests.

The mission of the socialist lawyers and judges is not to seek justice, but to use the judicial system to overturn the unjust and unfair laws, on behalf of their oppressed identity groups.

For socialists, there is no reality other than the total political reality of their socialist ideology, and for them, every act they perform is in the cause of promoting their socialist utopia.

This explains part of their intolerance of any right of free speech that is contrary to their socialist ideology. The political correct intolerance is the first stage of political repression that only the official state-sanctioned version of the truth is tolerated.

For socialists, the end goal of converting America into a global socialist state justifies lying, under all conditions.

Truth, for socialists, means allegiance to their socially-constructed reality. When other socialists affirm the lies and propaganda, the intensity of their belief in their truth increases.

In contrast, the truth content of a statement, for conservatives, is the correspondence of the statement with the facts. Correspondence with facts means that another person "sees" the observable facts, and verifies the validity of the correspondence with the facts.

For example, Representative Adam Schiff has said that the Nunes Republican memo is false, because the Nunes memo denies that Trump collaborated with Russia to deny Hillary the Presidency.

The differences about the truth content of the Nunes memo versus the Schiff Democrat memo are irreconcilable.

The truth content of the dossier, for Schiff, depends on whether it is consistent with the Democrat's socially constructed reality that Trump stole the election from the rightful winner.

To Schiff, the Nunes memo is false and the dossier is truth because the premises of the dossier confirms his prior conviction.

The truth content of the dossier acts as the logical confirmation of Trump's guilt. The contents of the dossier act as the evidence for the Democrat's conclusion that Trump is an illegitimate President, and must be removed from office.

For Schiff, the truth content of the dossier is not a mistaken conclusion, it is an article of their religious ideology of socialism. For them, the dossier is the truth.

The truth of Schiff's reality rests in how the dossier promotes his concept of social justice. His truth is confirmed by how many other socialists demonstrate extreme allegiance to their socialist religion.

When Schiff makes his statements about the truth of the dossier, 65 million Democrat voters confirm the "truth" content of Schiff's assertion.

When Feinstein claims that Kavanaugh is a rapist, 65 million Democrat voters affirm the truth of her allegation.

Nothing will change Schiff's mind because his belief system requires him to embrace the socially-constructed truth that America is a flawed and racist nation.

In Schiff's belief system, only a socialist elite, like Schiff, is capable of correcting the original sin of slavery by imposing their brand of a totalitarian state.

Unless, and until, conservatives cross their mental Rubicon, the insane behavior of Schiff is exactly what conservatives can expect from Democrats.

In the process of adjusting their mental image of Democrats, natural rights conservatives must jettison the idea that socialist Democrats share the American moral belief in the rule of law.

Prior to the election of Obama, American citizens shared a widely-held common definition about truth, reality, and rationality.

The common definition of truth and objectivity was rooted in Western Civilization traditions of scientific realism and empirical observation.

Prior to Obama, obedience to the rule of law was based upon shared cultural values of individual freedom and liberty.

After Obama was elected, obedience to the rule of law was based upon allegiance to the enduring socialist cultural values of class and race conflict.

For example, before Obama, if a common citizen shared her email server with foreign agents, as Hillary did, then predicable results would mean that the common citizen would bear the same application of justice, as Hillary.

Conversely, if Hillary escapes justice, then there is no rationale for common citizens to obey the rule of law.

In the corrupt centralized tyranny, the elites hold themselves above the law. The agents of the deep state in the FBI, and Department of Justice protect the elites from the equal application of the law.

The social and cultural values of the Democrat socialists do not connect at any point with the cultural and social values of natural rights conservatives.

On every single principle of a natural rights republic, the socialists have an alien, subversive, view of America.

In the absence of voluntary allegiance to obey the rule of law, conservatives must find an alternative moral principle to deal with socialists during the period of civil dissolution.

The replacement moral value is to apply the ancient religious code of behavior:

> In all things whatsoever ye would that men should do to you, do ye even so to them.

The moral command of natural rights conservatives is to treat socialists exactly as the socialists treat conservatives:

> Do unto others, as you would have them do to you.

> Do unto others as they do unto you.

Moral behavior, in the treatment of socialists, means crossing the mental Rubicon to understand that the American representative republic is over.

Conservatives must confront the socialist Democrats as the enemies to liberty that they are.

And, treat them as Caesar treated the corrupt tyranny in Rome, after he crossed the Rubicon.

The organizational entity of the new political party that manages the transition from the Former United States to the Democratic Republic of America is called the Citizens Liberty Party, (CLP).

The mission of the Citizens Liberty Party is to lead a national political movement that creates a new states-rights union, that restores the linkage between the Declaration of Independence, and the Constitution of the Democratic Republic of America.

The CLP is organized into 250 metro regional chapters, whose leadership is drawn from the local CLP Leadership Alliance.

The local political units organize elections and policies that serve citizens in each region during the transition from the Former United States to the new Democratic Republic of America.

Chapter 10.
Correcting Madison's Flawed Rules of Ratification.

The new Constitution of the Democratic Republic of America must be ratified by the citizens in the states that choose to join the Union.

Parts of Madison's ratification process can serve as a guide to the ratification process. The first part of the ratification process is the call for a convention of the states.

It is an incontrovertible historical fact that Madison, and the legislature of Virginia, called for the constitutional convention to "fix" the Articles of Confederation.

Rather than "fixing" the Articles, Madison intended to implement an entirely new, centralized government.

There were only 12 self-selected wealthy elites, and only five states, that responded to Madison's resolution.

The Congress, so assembled at the time, had nothing to do with Madison's initial call for a convention, and the Congress, today, has no legal or moral authority to stop states from abolishing the current form of government.

The purpose of the convention of states is to manage the citizen's referendum in each state that provides citizens with a choice of 3 constitutional options:

> 1. Allow the citizens of a state to vote to maintain its membership in the current U. S. constitutional framework, to be called the Former United States.
> 2. Allow the citizens to vote to join the Socialist States of America, in confederation with California.
> 3. Allow the citizens to join the Democratic Republic of America, the new natural rights republic.

As described by Luther Martin during the debates over the rules for ratification, common citizens would not ratify the Constitution, "unless they were hurried into it by surprise."

Madison's political strategy was to adopt rules of ratification that manipulated the vote on ratification, and hurry the vote in illegitimate conventions, to avoid defeat.

His political strategy of hurrying the vote was a success. Without discussion or debate, five states immediately ratified the Constitution.

Madison's rules for ratification adopted by the Convention, however, provide a concrete historical precedent of an illegitimate ratification process.

Madison's rules of ratification evaded the legitimate authority of the state legislatures, in favor of a ratification process of self-appointed elites.

Madison used this part of Locke's ideas about excluding irrational citizens in his constitutional rules of 1787, when he eliminated the ability of common citizens, (howling masses) from participating in the institutional arrangement of his separation of powers.

During the debates over how his constitution would be ratified, he embraced exclusion of common citizens in reading about the deliberations, and excluding them from the ratification process.

As he noted on June 12, if common citizens "possessed information about the Constitution," who knows what they would do with the information?

It was a better idea, said Madison, that only the "influential class of citizens," be allowed to have access to information, in order to avoid the influence of the "unreflecting multitude."

As Jackson Turner Main stated,

> Since the Federalists were a minority in at least six and probably seven states, they ought surely to have been defeated. Yet they came from behind to win. Why?

According to Main, 75 delegates to the various state ratification conventions were opposed to ratification, yet in the secret balloting, their votes were changed to voting for the Constitution.

From Madison's notes,

June 12.

In Committee of the Whole, — The question was taken on the fifteenth Resolution, to wit, referring the new system to the people of the United States for ratification. It passed in the affirmative, — Massachusetts, Pennsylvania, Virginia, North Carolina, South Carolina, Georgia, aye — 6; Connecticut, New York, New Jersey, no — 3; Delaware, Maryland, divided.

"15. Resolved, that the amendments which shall be offered to the Confederation, by the Convention, ought, at a proper time or times, after the approbation of Congress, to be submitted to an assembly or assemblies of representatives, recommended by the several Legislatures, to be expressly chosen by the people to consider and decide thereon."

Mr. MADISON observed, that, if the opinions of the people were to be our guide, it would be difficult to say what course we ought to take. No member of the Convention could say what the opinions of his constituents were at this time; much less could he say what they would think, if possessed of the information and lights possessed by the members here; and still less, what would be their way of thinking six or twelve months hence.

We ought to consider what was right and necessary in itself for the attainment of a proper government. A plan adjusted to this idea will recommend itself. The respectability of this Convention will give weight to their recommendation of it. Experience will be constantly urging the adoption of it; and all the most enlightened and respectable citizens will be its advocates. Should we fall short of the necessary and proper point, this influential class of citizens will be turned against the plan, and little support in opposition to them can be gained to it from the unreflecting multitude.

Mr. GERRY repeated his opinion that it was necessary to consider what the people would approve. This had been the policy of all legislators. If the reasoning (of Mr. MADISON) were just, and we supposed a limited monarchy the best form in itself, we ought to recommend it, though the genius of the people was decidedly adverse to it, and, having no hereditary distinctions among us, we were destitute of the essential materials for such an innovation.

On August 12, Madison again voted to keep the records of the debate secret.

From Madison's notes,

August 11.

On the question on the words to follow, to wit, "except such parts thereof as may in their judgment require secrecy," — Massachusetts, Connecticut, New Jersey, Virginia, North Carolina, Georgia, aye, — 6; Pennsylvania, Delaware, Maryland, South Carolina, no, — 4; New Hampshire divided.

Again, on September 17, the last day of the Convention, without discussion or debate, Madison promoted the idea of destroying the record of the Convention entirely.

From Madison's notes,

September 17.

Mr. KING suggested that the Journals of the Convention should be either destroyed, or deposited in the custody of the President. He thought, if suffered to be made public, a bad use would be made of them by those who would wish to prevent the adoption of the Constitution.

Mr. WILSON preferred the second expedient. He had at one time liked the first best; but as false suggestions may be propagated, it should not be made impossible to contradict them.

A question was then put on depositing the Journals, and other papers of the Convention, in the hands of the President; on which, —

New Hampshire, Massachusetts, Connecticut, New Jersey, Pennsylvania, Delaware, Virginia, North Carolina, South Carolina, Georgia, aye, — 10; Maryland,4 no, — 1.

The President, having asked what the Convention meant should be done with the Journals, &c., whether copies were to be allowed to the members, if applied for, it was resolved, nem. con. "that he retain the Journal and other papers, subject to the order of Congress, if ever formed under the Constitution."

Madison's logic for keeping the deliberations secret and for evading the legitimate rules then in place, under the Articles, was explained by Madison on August 30.

The rules for ratification would allow the elites to pull a fast one over the common citizens, or as Madison stated, "over the whole body of the people."

From Madison's notes,

August 30.

Mr. MADISON remarked, that if the blank should be filled with "seven," "eight," or "nine," the Constitution as it stands, might be put in force over the whole body of the people, though less than a majority of them should ratify it.

The two parts of Madison's ratification strategy were to keep the common citizens in the dark, and to place the ratification process in the hands of the corrupt elites, at the state level, who used their corrupt power to change the votes on the ratification.

The entire ratification process, debated on August 30 is about the minimal number of state conventions required to ratify.

Madison suggested that just 7 states would be required. The part about the number of states required had been left blank, and the debate that day revolved around that issue.

As Mr. King noted, the rules for ratification would allow a minority to impose a government on the majority:

Mr. KING thought this amendment necessary; otherwise, as the Constitution now stands, it will operate on the whole, though ratified by a part only.

The next day, in a precursor to the 10th amendment debate, King attempted to limit the operation of the central government to only the states which ratified it.

In Convention. — Mr. KING moved to add to the end of Article 21, the words, "between the said States;" so as to confine the operation of the Government to the States ratifying it.

The hidden agenda of Madison's ratification strategy was exposed on August 31, in the debate between King and Gouverneur Morris.

From Madison's notes,

August 31.

Mr. GOUVERNEUR MORRIS thought the blank ought to be filled in a two-fold way, so as to provide for the event of the ratifying States being contiguous, which would render a smaller number sufficient; and the event of their being dispersed, which would require a greater number for the introduction of the Government.

Mr. GOUVERNEUR MORRIS moved to strike out, "conventions of the," after "ratifications;" leaving the States to pursue their own modes of ratification.

Mr. KING thought that striking out "conventions," as the requisite mode, was equivalent to giving up the business altogether. Conventions alone, which will avoid all the obstacles from the complicated formation of the Legislatures, will succeed; and if not positively required by the plan, its enemies will oppose that mode.

Mr. GOUVERNEUR MORRIS said, he meant to facilitate the adoption of the plan, by leaving the modes approved by the several State Constitutions to be followed.

In other words, Morris disclosed that Madison's entire ratification process was designed to gain illegitimate approval in a procedure under the control of the elites in each state. Morris thought the elites in each state should do whatever they wanted to do.

King responded that the amendment was equivalent to giving up on a legitimate ratification process.

As explained by Martin, the ratification process would fail, unless common citizens were, "hurried into it by surprise."

Mr. L. MARTIN believed Mr. MORRIS to be right, that after a while the people would be against it; but for a different reason from that alleged. He believed they would not ratify it, unless hurried into it by surprise.

From Madison's notes,

August 31.

Mr. MADISON considered it best to require Conventions; among other reasons for this, that the powers given to the General Government being taken from the State Governments, the Legislatures would be more disinclined than Conventions composed in part at least of other men; and if disinclined, they could devise modes apparently promoting, but really thwarting, the ratification. The difficulty in Maryland was no greater than in other States, where no mode of change was pointed out by the Constitution, and all officers were under oath to support it. The people were, in fact, the fountain of all power, and by resorting to them, all difficulties were got over. They could alter constitutions as they pleased. It was a principle in the Bills of Rights, that first principles might be resorted to.

Mr. L. MARTIN insisted on a reference to the State Legislatures. He urged the danger of commotions from a resort to the people and to first principles; in which the Government might be on one side, and the people on the other. He was apprehensive of no such consequences, however, in Maryland, whether the Legislature or the people should be appealed to. Both of them would be generally against the Constitution. He repeated also the peculiarity in the Maryland Constitution.

On August 31, the ratification process was amended twice.

From Madison's notes,

August 31.

Article 21, as amended, was then agreed to by all the States, Maryland excepted, and Mr. JENIFER being aye.

Article 22 was then taken up, to wit: "This Constitution shall be laid before the United States in Congress assembled, for their approbation; and it is the opinion of this Convention that it should be afterwards submitted to a Convention chosen in each State, under the recommendation of its Legislature, in order to receive the ratification of such Convention."

Mr. GOUVERNEUR MORRIS and Mr. PINCKNEY moved to strike out the words, "for their approbation."

On this question, —

New Hampshire, Connecticut, New Jersey,1 Pennsylvania, Delaware, Virginia, North Carolina, South Carolina, aye, — 8; Massachusetts, Maryland, Georgia, no, — 3.

Mr. GOUVERNEUR MORRIS and Mr. PINCKNEY then moved to amend the article so as to read:

"This Constitution shall be laid before the United States in Congress assembled; and it is the opinion of this Convention, that it should afterwards be submitted to a Convention chosen in each State, in order to receive the ratification of such Convention; to which end the several Legislatures ought to provide for the calling Conventions within their respective States as speedily as circumstances will permit."

Mr. GOUVERNEUR MORRIS said his object was to impress in stronger terms the necessity of calling Conventions, in order to prevent enemies to the plan from giving it the go by. When it first appears, with the sanction of this Convention, the people will be favorable to it. By degrees the State officers, and those interested in the State Governments, will intrigue, and turn the popular current against it.

Luther Marin was so disgusted by the deception and deceit in the ratification debate that he left the convention.

The final version of ratification, adopted on September 15, omitted the text of the amendment, on August 31.

The delegates never had a chance to see the final version of the ratification rules before they were engraved as the Constitution.

Rather than the amendment voted on August 31, the text in the Constitution reads:

Article VII.

The ratification of the conventions of nine States shall be sufficient for the establishment of this Constitution between the States so ratifying the same.

Done in Convention, by the unanimous consent of the States present, the 17th day of September, in the year of our Lord 1787, and of the independence of the United States of America, the twelfth. In witness whereof, we have hereunto subscribed our names.

The text about unanimous consent was a lie, since New York did not have authorized delegates there, and the text of the amendment to place it before the Congress was omitted entirely.

Part of Madison's deception was submitting the draft of the Constitution and its rules in different documents to Congress, without any instruction to Congress on what it was to do with the draft.

As a result of the indecision created by the submission of multiple documents, Congress simply sent part of the documents of the draft Constitution to the states without any instructions on what the states should do.

The self-appointed elites in the various states adopted their own rules to ratify the document, including the force and fraud of arresting delegates in Pennsylvania, who were trying to leave the fraudulent proceedings.

The Federalists held them, against their will, so that the convention had the patina of a quorum.

As correctly predicted by Elbridge Gerry, Madison's Constitution precipitated a civil war, and ended in a centralized elite tyranny that is disconnected from the consent of the governed.

From Madison's notes,

September 17.

Mr. GERRY described the painful feelings of his situation, and the embarrassments under which he rose to offer any further observations on the subject which had been finally decided. Whilst the plan was depending, he had treated it with all the freedom he thought it deserved. He now felt himself bound, as he was disposed, to treat it with the respect due to the act of the Convention.

He hoped he should not violate that respect in declaring, on this occasion, his fears that a civil war may result from the present crisis of the United States. In Massachusetts, particularly, he saw the danger of this calamitous event. In that State there are two parties, one devoted to Democracy, the worst, he thought, of all political evils; the other as violent in the opposite extreme. From the collision of these in opposing and resisting the Constitution, confusion was greatly to be feared. He had thought it necessary, for this and other reasons, that the plan should have been proposed in a more mediating shape, in order to abate the heat and opposition of parties. As it had been passed by the Convention, he was persuaded it would have a contrary effect. He could not, therefore, by signing the Constitution, pledge himself to abide by it at all events. The proposed form made no difference with him. But if it were not otherwise apparent, the refusals to sign should never be known from him. Alluding to the remarks of Doctor FRANKLIN, he could not, he said, but view them as levelled at himself and the other gentlemen who meant not to sign.

In contrast to Madison's flawed ratification process, the Democratic Republic of America Constitution outlines a simple, democratic process.

Article IV. Admission of New States and Removal of States From the Union.

Upon a petition for admission from a state legislature, new states may be admitted by the Senate into this Union.

The Senate may determine the geographical area and jurisdiction of a new State, including partial jurisdictions of states not currently a member of this Union.

Verified citizens of a partial jurisdiction in any state not in the Union may petition the Senate based upon a certified referendum of 66% of the citizens in the proposed jurisdiction.

Prior to their admission to the Union, as a condition of admission, the state or partial jurisdiction, seeking admission must deposit a full year of their projected taxes into the National Treasury, as determined by the Senate.

Chapter 11.
The Democratic Republic of America.

The nation is split along ideological and geographical lines. The graphic below, describes that socialists live on the east and west coasts, while Trump voters live in the other states.

Map of U. S. Voters, by County, 2016 Presidential Election.

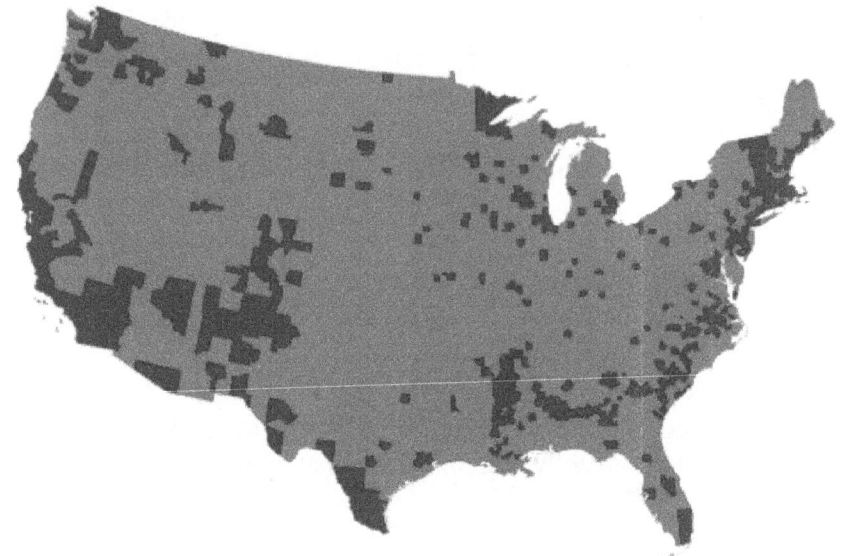

Credit: M. E. J. Newman, University of Michigan, 2016.

The differences between conservatives and Democrat socialists are irreconcilable. There are no common national values that bind the socialist citizens together with natural rights conservatives, in a common national mission.

In the absence of shared cultural values, the nation has lost the voluntary allegiance to the rule of law.

The end goal of the Articles of Confederation, in the nation's first constitution, was individual freedom.

The end goal of the Democratic Republic of America is protection of individual freedom.

The creation of the Democratic Republic of America, today, requires a cadre of leaders who look and act like the 37 elite Federalists, who signed Madison's Constitution.

Madison's document is defective because it did not establish a common national mission. Rather, Madison's Constitution is simply a set of civil rules of procedure to adjudicate class conflicts between the natural aristocracy and the common citizens.

Beginning with the global trade acts of the early 1990s, the Republicans used their elected authority in Washington to derive maximum financial benefits for themselves by attaching the Republican's own private utility function to the financial utility function of the global corporate special interests.

Eventually, the Republicans abandoned their original social class interests in America, and became citizens of the world.

The reason they have never pushed back against leftist ideology is that an ideological battle with socialist Democrats does not promote the Republican interests in a one-world global government.

Since 1992, corporate net income has increased dramatically, while the average American household income has declined dramatically.

This outcome in income disparity is a result of the Republican economic policies. The term used by Republicans to cover their deceit is "free trade."

The mission of the leaders of the Citizens Liberty Party is to replace the Republican "free trade" fraud and Madison's unfair rules of civil procedure by re-directing the new Democratic Republic of America back to the principles of government in the Declaration of Independence.

Following the precedent set by Madison for overthrowing the Articles of Confederation, the Citizens Liberty Party would organize and manage the creation of a shadow government of The Democratic Republic of America.

As Madison's example demonstrates, it will likely take about 6 years of operating the shadow government, during the transition period, before the individual state legislatures are ready to ratify the new constitution.

Elected representatives in the various state legislatures, today, would serve a similar dual role during the transition period to the state ratification of the Constitution of the Democratic Republic of America.

The elected representatives would serve on the shadow government committees, and also shepherd the ratification process in their states, before the citizens voted in a referendum to join the new nation, stay with the Former United States, or confederate with the new Socialist States of America.

Some of the elected representatives would also serve in the U.S. Congress, during the transition, to establish the laws and process of the national civil dissolution.

Part of the mission of the leaders of the Citizens Liberty Party, during the period of transition, is to re-direct the economic and banking policies of Madison, which served elite interests, to serving the national sovereign economic interests.

The work during the transition is based upon three important economic principles:

Sovereign nations have an identifiable national welfare function.

Sovereign nations have an identifiable set of factor endowments that establish a comparative advantage in production with trading partners.

Economic and financial policies can identify and implement laws that maximize the national welfare function.

In other words, the work during the transition period is to identify and implement a unique set of cultural and political values in America that enable citizens to obtain maximum individual liberty, and which allow citizens to pursue their happiness.

The common name of this set of American cultural values is "the natural rights republic." The values of natural rights binds citizens into a common national mission of preserving and protecting natural rights.

In contrast to the cultural values of natural rights, Madison substituted the British social class political model of economic policy.

The reward structure associated with Madison's collectivist rules (We, the people), about income distribution have been manipulated to the benefit of the most powerful set of elites who obtain power over setting the rules and the laws.

Madison's economy did not bind citizens to a common national mission, and the end result of Madison's system is a centralized elite tyranny.

George Washington chose Alexander Hamilton as the treasury secretary. Hamilton implemented the precursor of the modern global corporate banking system.

Hamilton created the unconstitutional First Bank, the so-called Bank of the United States. The first Bank was a replica of the Bank of England, which was designed to serve the financial interests of the British nobility and upper classes.

The ownership of the First Bank was in the hand of wealthy global bankers. Their mission in operating the bank was to reward themselves, and their banks, through manipulation of interest rates and the money supply.

Their management of the Bank led to a wildly unstable economic system that collapsed about every 10 years, due to speculation and insider greed.

In order to insure the banker's allegiance, Hamilton's first act as Treasurer was to re-issue new government bonds that were bought at a discount by the wealthy global bankers, who owned the First Bank.

Hamilton promised the new investors that he would redeem the discounted bonds at full face value, creating unearned, risk-free, windfall profits for the wealthy investors.

Part of Hamilton's swindle of common citizens was to use his scheme to make the initial "Revolutionary War Bonds" held by soldiers and farmers worthless.

As a counter-measure to Hamilton's elitist proposal, Madison proposed that Congress should set aside some money for the original owners of the Revolutionary War Bonds, who tended to be ordinary Americans and not new investors and speculators.

Madison's idea failed to be enacted.

On a political and pragmatic level Madison's idea would have been difficult to implement. Nearly half the members of Congress had invested in Hamilton's First Bank bonds. The elected representatives stood to benefit financially from Hamilton's plan.

Sharing financial benefits with farmers and soldiers would, as a result of Madison's idea, would not have been valuable to the Federalist elites who dominated Congress at the time.

The insider elites benefiting from insider trading, at the creation of the First Bank, is the precursor of the modern day swamp, which only benefits the elites in Washington.

Hamilton's economic policies reflected a unique set of cultural values that served to benefit the elites, just like his model, the Bank of England.

Different institutional arrangements in the apparatus of government, and different configurations of constitutional rights, produce different rates of economic growth and income creation.

Given a certain type of prior social and political conditions in political power and cultural values, the economy created by Hamilton could have taken a different economic trajectory.

There is only one constitutional configuration that produces maximum economic growth, based upon maximum rates of knowledge creation and diffusion.

That constitutional configuration is the natural rights republic because it starts out with the assumption that the function of government economic policies is to create "maximum" happiness for citizens.

No other constitutional configuration starts out with this social goal.

The banking and financial system in the Democratic Republic of America must create the rules for maximum rates of capital investment in the new technological combinations and innovations.

The major task of the Citizen Liberty Party, during the period of transition, is to find the single "best" national social welfare function, based upon the nation's initial factor endowments. Then, to lay out the policies and programs that will achieve that national welfare function.

The function of the economic and financial constitutional rules is to organize these concepts into a coherent set of constitutional rules that citizens of the Democratic Republic voluntarily agree to follow, based upon their level of trust that other citizens will also follow the rules.

The voluntary allegiance to the rule of law in the Democratic Republic of America is based upon the belief that all citizens benefit from rule obedience, and all citizens have an equal economic opportunity to gain financial success.

The task of the CLP shadow banking system is to create an economy of maximum economic growth. Maximum growth means changing Hamilton's institutional configuration from unearned rewards in asset speculation, for the elites to rewards for investors and savers, from a capital investment configuration in each state and metro region.

The central banking system of Hamilton would be replaced by a decentralized capital market system that promotes maximum rates of capital investments in each state economy.

During the period of transition, the shadow banking system of the Democratic Republic of America must identify that national welfare function which stimulates increased rates of capital investment.

During and after the economic collapse of 2008, Fed Chairman Bernanke exercised unlimited, unchecked power to use government money to bail out global and domestic financial institutions.

Bernake directed $85 billion to the insurance giant, AIG, and $700 billion to other global banks and corporations.

On a Friday afternoon, Bernake said, "If we don't do this today we won't have an economy on Monday."

Bernake's figure of $700 billion in bailouts is fake news. The 2011 Special Inspector General's report for the bailout stated that the total commitment of government bailouts was $16.8 trillion dollars, not the more modest $700 billion promoted by Bernake.

Common citizens in America can be forgiven for the mistaken assumption that the Fed's actions of frittering away $17 trillion in public money were aimed at protecting the national sovereign economic interest.

Under the rule of law in a representative republic, common citizens assume that all citizens have allegiance to obey the rule of law. The common citizens assumed that Bernake shared their allegiance to the rule of law, when, in fact, the rule of law does not extend to the financial elites.

Bernake had no allegiance to the rule of law, or to protecting the national sovereign economic interest. His bailout was simply and solely an effort to bail out the global banks, as a part of his effort to stabilize the global banking system.

Bernake protected the financial interests of the global banking community because Bernake is a corporate globalist, who owes his allegiance to the world, not to U. S. citizens.

At the same time of Bernake's bailout, the big banks, like JP Morgan, were using their investment trading desk to place "short selling" bets against the sovereign national economic interests. In other words, the banks were betting against the American economy surviving the collapse.

At the same time that foreign banks, like HSBC, were obtaining government money from the bailout, they were engaged in money laundering $881 billion for the Mexican drug cartels.

At the same time Goldman Saks obtained bailout money, they were trading inside information to Raj Rajaratnam, who was making $1 million, per minute, in corrupt insider trading profits.

The story of the Fed's corruption, under Bernake, would have remained a secret if not forced by a Congressional audit, in 2011, that revealed that Bernake allowed the banks to use the money for any purpose they chose, including not having to pay the money back to the Fed.

The Fed operates in secret, and is not accountable to the consent of the governed. This 2011 audit was the first, and last, in the Fed's 100 year history.

To paraphrase George Mason University constitutional economist, James Buchanan, the welfare function that the Fed maximized with the bailout were the global banks, not the sovereign national welfare.

From a historical perspective, the behavior of the Fed during the 2008 collapse is precisely the same behavior it conducts every 10 years to bail out the corrupt U. S. banking system. The collapse of 2008 was caused by the Fed's irrational money creation and interest rate schemes.

The money creation caused inflation, and stimulated asset speculation in worthless housing mortgage bonds. The network of global bank engaged in insider trading and asset speculation, which caused the financial bubble of 2008.

The scenario of 2008 was just like all the other economic collapses caused by the unstable economic system implemented by Hamilton.

The flaw in Hamilton's arrangement traces back to Madison's flawed constitution that does not state a national economic goal. Like the Constitution, the Fed does not have a mission to protect the national sovereign interest, and the Fed operates outside the authority of any consent of the governed.

Madison's Constitution was designed to reward the financial elites with his institutional arrangement of power, and Hamilton's First Bank, the Second Bank, all the way to the

Fed, is simply one tool the elites in the swamp use to reward themselves with government money.

The operational funds to operate the Fed are not from Congressional appropriations, they are from internal corporate profits, generated by the Fed in conducting its operations.

The revenue model of the Fed is risk-free and foolproof, and guarantees a net profit, every year.

First, the Fed creates money that is backed only by "promise to pay" as legal tender.

Next, the Fed uses the worthless money to buy its own bonds, that are guaranteed to mature at a profit. The Fed sells its bonds to its global banking partners, making profits on the sale of debt.

The profits from the Feds operations are then used by the Fed to provide the monetary reserves for the nation's banking system, so that the banks will not go belly-up when they engage in risky speculative loans.

The Fed conducts this lucrative business model through one of its operational divisions, called the Open Market Committee, a secret insider trading system between the Fed and global banks.

The Fed imposes discipline on member banks by regulatory oversight, setting reserve requirements, which forces banks to buy the Fed's bonds, and its manipulation of interest rates.

The federal funds rate is another secret, insider trading system that sets the rate of interest that member banks loan money to each other. The loans are guaranteed to make a profit, which encourages speculation.

Changes in the federal funds rate triggers a chain of economic and financial events that eventually lead to an economic collapse about every ten years.

The Federal funds rate is linked to the operations of a global banking cartel that controls economic conditions in all world governments.

Nothing about the Fed's activities are under the legitimate authority of the consent of the governed. The operations of the Federal Open Market Committee do not require approval by the President or anyone else in the executive or legislative branches of government.

Nothing in Madison's separation of power checks or balances the operations of the Fed. After the leadership is appointed by the President, the leaders, like Bernake, are free to do whatever pleases them.

What pleases the Fed's leadership the most is pleasing the global banks that own the ownership shares in the Fed. The ownership interests in the Fed are the member banks of the global banking cartel.

These global banks include:
- Rothschild Bank of London,
- Warburg Bank of Hamburg,
- Rothschild Bank of Berlin,
- Lehman Brothers of New York,
- Lazard Brothers of Paris,
- Kuhn Loeb Bank of New York,
- Israel Moses Seif Banks of Italy,
- Goldman, Sachs of New York,
- Warburg Bank of Amsterdam,
- Chase Manhattan Bank of New York.

Up until the Congressional audit of 2011, this list of global bankers who owned ownership interests in the Fed, was secret information.

The global banking cartel exercises unchecked, unelected and undelegated power over the U. S. economy through their power on the Fed's New York bank, which controls the creation of the nation's money supply in the 11 other Fed district banks.

In other words, one bank, the Fed's New York bank, is more powerful than all other 11 district banks, and the New York Bank is controlled by the global banking cartel.

Which explains why Bernake used the $17 trillion bailout to reward the global banking cartel.

The Federal Reserve, today, just like the First Bank, controls elected representatives in Congress by offering them insider financial rewards. In Hamilton's example, he used his discounted bonds to reward members of Congress with a guaranteed profit on the bonds that he issued.

Today, in a secret, sweetheart deal, the Fed offers part-time employment, on the weekends, to members of Congress. The Fed pays the members of Congress lucrative salaries and bonuses, for their part-time work.

Which explains how so many elected representatives arrive in Washington as paupers, and leave the swamp as multi-millionaires.

The new Democratic Republic of America requires a central bank, that performs some of the functions of the current Fed.

The task of the shadow banking system, during the period of transition, is to examine the defects of Hamilton's system, and offer solutions that places the operations of the Central Bank under the consent of the governed and mandates that the Central Bank maximize the nation's sovereign economic welfare function.

The threat to individual liberty today arises from a dedicated ideological, left-wing political movement that seeks to undermine a legitimate constitutional government, in order to implement a totalitarian socialist, centralized regime.

Like the Federalists, the socialists believe that they possess a moral quality that would allow them to make better decisions about society, in a modern form of "virtual representation."

The 65 million voters who voted for Hillary will continue to vote the socialist ticket because the Democrat Party has made those voters financially dependent on government welfare.

This outcome was clearly foreseen by the natural rights patriots at Madisons' Convention.

When 3 of the Massachusetts delegates to the Convention left Philadelphia, in disgust, they returned to their state to write out their objections to the document.

Malachi Maynard, Consider Arms, and Samuel Field, wrote that Madison's Constitution directly contradicted the natural rights of citizens guaranteed by their state constitution.

"What would keep common citizens from being enslaved by a constitution that rejected the principles of the revolution?" they asked.

They explained that while Madison's constitution guaranteed a republican form of government, it was a slavery-based representative republic.

The slaveocracy obtained 60% more representation in the House of Representatives than northern states, and the slave owners obtained constitutional protection in their property by forcing other states to return their runaway slaves.

The slaveocracy's numerical power in the House of Representatives, plus rules on import and export taxes on the products made by slaves, gave the southern states control over taxation and the nation's economic policies.

Madison wove slavery into the fabric of government, and his rules could easily be transfigured to incorporate a new form of socialist slavery today. Rather than being owned by a plantation elite, under Democrat socialism, common citizens would be owned by the government.

The natural rights conservatives are in the same position, today, as the colonists in 1765.

They are, as Franklin noted, "subjects of subjects."

As correctly analyzed, in 1764, by Rhode Island Governor Stephen Hopkins, the colonists, as subjects of the Crown, were just like slaves.

Hopkins wrote,

> Britain's glorious constitution guaranteed that no one ever be deprived of his property without his consent. On the contrary those who are governed by the will of another or of others, and whose property may be taken from them by taxes, or otherwise without their consent and against their will are in the same miserable condition of slaves.

Twelve years later, the colonists fought the King for their liberty.

Twelve years after that, Madison implemented a coup that embedded irrevocable, permanent institutional rules that empowered the slaveocracy, and opened the possibility that socialists would use the instrumental powers to impose a socialist tyranny.

In Madison's system of checks and balances, constitutional laws provide the institutional framework for a permanent advantage of the natural aristocracy.

The permanent advantage of the natural aristocracy can easily be converted to a permanent advantage of the Democrat socialists.

Since 2016, the socialist political strategy has been based entirely on the politics of hate. During the mid-term elections of 2018, the socialists did not adopt a traditional party platform that championed the financial interests of common citizens.

Rather, their entire strategy was to vilify their enemies.

The socialists are engaged in a vicious, violent campaign of hate against President Trump, and the common citizens who voted for Trump.

The Democrats have no sense of patriotism and allegiance to the nation.

Their intent is to replace individual liberty, itself, in order to substitute left-wing totalitarian collectivism. In their worldview individuals only exist as a member of an aggrieved group.

In other words, the left's target is the concept of individual liberty, and in order to destroy liberty, they must first destroy the existing Representative Republic.

One, or the other, legal philosophy, must be vanquished from the field of battle.

Natural Rights Conservatives need to come to grips with the new political reality of America.

As explained by Thomas Paine, the new American government must be built on the truth, moral truth, not on power relationships that existed in the mixed British class system that Madison palmed off on America in 1787.

For Paine, as for Jefferson, the truth was that God had granted citizens certain inalienable rights, commonly called "natural rights."

The new government, said Paine, "is derived solely from a sovereign people…mutually and reciprocally maintained principles of nature in society."

In crossing the Rubicon to create the Democratic Republic of America, natural rights conservatives must restore the principles in the Declaration of Independence that the "consent of the governed" is the glue that binds citizens together to obey the constitutional rules that they give to themselves.

It is imperative that the natural rights conservatives vanquish the Democrat socialists from the field of battle.

Chapter 12.
The Constitution of the Democratic Republic of America© 2018.

All rights reserved under Title 17, U.S. Code, International and Pan-American copyright Conventions. No part of this work may be reproduced or transmitted in any form or by any means, electronic or mechanical, including photocopying, scanning, recording or duplication by any information storage or retrieval system without prior written permission from the author, except for the inclusion of brief quotations with attribution in a review or report.

Preamble:

We, the citizens of the Democratic Republic of America, establish this constitutional contract between our respective states and the National Government of the Democratic Republic of America.

We solemnly swear and affirm that we establish this contract to preserve and protect the natural and civil rights of citizens in each state, and to protect and defend the sovereignty of each state and the nation, from foreign and domestic threats.

Guiding Principles of the National Government.

By freely and voluntarily joining our state government into the union of Democratic Republic, we affirm that the National Government will be guided by the following principles:

"…that all legitimate government authority is derived from the consent of the citizens governed…"

"…that those governed by the laws and whose individual freedom is restricted by the laws should have the greatest say and consent in making of the laws…"

"…that those who make the laws and give consent to the laws, acting as representatives of the citizens, bind themselves and their constituents to following the laws…"

"…that individual citizens who freely give their consent to form a government through constitutional conventions are bound by the original contract until the operation of the government becomes destructive to the original intent of obtaining individual freedom and the pursuit of happiness…"

"…that the parties to the constitutional contract are individual citizens acting through their elected representatives at the state and national levels of government…"

"…that the citizens of each state have mechanisms in place in the constitutional contract to modify or abolish the national government, including the right of each state to vote on remaining a member of the national government in a referendum to be held every 20 years from the date of admittance…"

"…that as the consequence of the sovereign authority of citizens, citizens have an inalienable natural right to remove an elected representative from office upon a referendum of 37% of registered voters in a state…"

"…that the National Government is instituted to allow individual citizens to pursue individual happiness and to limit the arbitrary application of government power over the lives of individuals…"

"…that the National Government that is created by this union of states shall never usurp the sovereign power or authority of the individual states or the sovereignty of the citizens in each state and that states have an inalienable right to call a convention of the states, without Congressional approval, to modify, amend, or abolish this Constitutional Contract."

"…that an individual's private property obtained through legal contract and title transfer, their rights to appropriate income and profits from the use of their private property, and their rights to dispose and transfer their private property are inviolate and derived from natural rights granted to them by

God, and that no government or constitutional contract may ever abrogate or subordinate these natural individual rights..."

"...that a citizens Grand Jury of 18 citizens is impaneled, for a term of 12 months, to protect and preserve the rights of citizens against the arbitrary application of government power against citizens..."

"...that a citizens Grand Jury of 18 citizens must inspect all national penal facilities within its district every 6 months, and report their findings to the Chief District Judge, who shall act to remedy the deficiencies found by the Grand Jury..."

"...that the 1776 American Revolution was ordained by God to allow citizens to pursue individual human freedoms and liberty from oppression and is an exceptional model in human history..."

"...that all citizens are created by God with equal natural rights, and that the purpose of the Nation is to protect the equal application of the law to all citizens, regardless of race or religious beliefs..."

Citizen Bill of Rights of the Democratic Republic of America.

We affirm and swear that all citizens in each of the respective Democratic Republic of America are guaranteed equal rights for all, and special privileges for none. Among them are:

1. That all citizens are due the equal application of justice and that no citizen is entitled to special or unequal treatment of the application of the law.

2. That all citizens have a natural right to worship and exercise their own religion and that the National Government is prohibited from making and enforcing any law respecting the establishment of an official national religion and compelling citizens to worship a national religion.

3. That all citizens have a natural right to truthful and honest statements from government agents and from elected representatives, and that it is the duty of the free press to report the truth.

4. That all citizens in the respective states have a natural right to own and use weapons, and that the National Government shall make no laws which abridge the right of law-abiding citizens from owning, keeping and bearing weapons.

5. That citizens have a civil right of action against elected representatives or agents of the National Government, for violation of the natural rights of citizens, upon a presentation of a motion of grievance to a Grand Jury of 18 citizens, who shall hear the case and determine the outcome and set the penalties for the violation by a majority vote.

6. No citizen in any state shall be seized or imprisoned, or stripped of his rights or possessions, or outlawed or exiled, or deprived of his standing in any other way, nor shall agents of the government proceed with force against him, or send others to do so, except by the lawful judgment of a true bill of indictment by a majority vote of a grand jury of 18 citizens, or by the rules of judicial civil procedure of the National Government.

7. The National Government shall be prohibited from making or enforcing any law that restricts the natural right of a citizen's freedom of speech and freedom of conscience.

8. The National Government is prohibited from making or enforcing any law which restricts the right of citizens to peaceably assemble, and to petition the National Government for a redress of grievances.

9. The National Government is prohibited from using agents of government or national resources to conduct searches and seizures of private citizen documents, and that

the documents obtained from illegal searches and seizures are inadmissible in any national court.

10.   The National Government, and every State government, are prohibited from making or enforcing any law which shall abridge the privileges or immunities of citizens of the Democratic Republic of America; nor shall any State deprive any person of life, liberty, or property, without due process of law; nor deny to any person within its jurisdiction the equal protection of the laws.

11.   No citizen shall be deprived of life, liberty, or property, without due process of law; nor shall private property be taken for public use, without just compensation, determined by a majority vote of a Grand Jury of 18 citizens.

12.   That all citizens are judged innocent until proven guilty in a trial of due process.

13.   No warrants or judicial orders in any criminal investigation shall be issued by a national court, except upon probable cause, determined in a judicial hearing, supported by an oath or affirmation of the government agent describing the specific items or locations to be searched and a judicial description of the crime being investigated.

14.   No person shall be held to answer for a capital, or otherwise infamous crime, unless on a presentment or indictment of a majority vote of a Grand Jury of 18 citizens who conduct an inquiry into the legitimacy of the government's allegation of a national crime.

15.   No citizen shall be subject for the same offence to be twice put in jeopardy of life or limb; nor shall be compelled in any criminal case to be a witness against himself.

16.   In all criminal prosecutions, the accused shall enjoy the right to a speedy and public trial, by an impartial jury of the State and district wherein the crime shall have been committed, which district shall have been previously

ascertained by law, and to be informed of the nature and cause of the accusation; to be confronted with the witnesses against him; to have compulsory process for obtaining witnesses in his favor, and to have the assistance of counsel for his defense.

17. The right of trial by jury shall be preserved, and no fact tried by a jury, shall be otherwise re-examined in any Court of the Democratic Republic of America, than according to the rules of the common law then obtaining in the national judiciary.

18. Excessive bail shall not be required, nor excessive fines imposed, nor cruel and unusual punishments inflicted, nor imprisonment for longer than 5 days, in the absence of specific charges and allegation of crime.

19. The Citizens Grand Jury in any State retains the right of initiating a citizen initiative on legislative proposals by a petition to the House of Representatives, which must respond to the petition within 30 days of receipt.

20. The right of citizens of the Democratic Republic America to vote, hold elected office, or deliberate in public debates, shall not be denied or abridged by the National Government or by any State on account of race, color of skin, sex, or religious beliefs.

Article I. The National Congress.

Section 1.

All legitimate authority of the National Government and the expression of the consent of the governed, is vested in the National Congress of the Democratic Republic of America, which shall consist of a Senate and House of Representatives.

No elected representative of the National Government may serve more than two consecutive terms, in the same office, nor more than 10 years in the same office, in a lifetime.

No law varying the compensation for the services of the Senators and Representatives shall take effect during an interval of 10 years.

All elected representatives of the National Government and all senior civil servants and agents are subject to the same laws and welfare benefits as common citizens who are bound by the laws made by the National Government.

Section 2. The Authority of the House of Representatives.

The House of Representatives shall represent the interests and rights of citizens in each state.

The elected representatives are chosen every fourth year by the verified citizens of the several States.

No elected representative may serve more than two terms in the same office, nor more than 10 years in the same office, during a lifetime.

No person shall be a representative who shall not have attained the age of twenty one, and shall have been a citizen of the Democratic Republic of America, for the previous 10 years, and who shall have been a resident of that State for the previous 10 years.

Each state shall have at least one representative. The total number of representatives shall not exceed one for every fifty thousand verified citizens.

The members of the House shall prepare the districts for representation based upon the criteria of compact geographical rectangular shapes, every 10 years, based upon a census and enumeration of citizens in each state.

Direct Taxes shall be apportioned among the several States according to their respective numbers of verified citizens. The House of Representatives sets the tax rate, pursuant to the budget transmitted to the House from the Senate.

The House has the exclusive power to charter and regulate a system of national banks designed to promote interstate and international commerce and maximum rates of economic growth among all Democratic Republic. The House imposes restrictions on the domain of power and authority of the system of national banks, and restricts the domain of the bank's authority to promote the economic welfare of sovereign Democratic Republic and sovereign citizens.

The House has the exclusive authority to regulate the issuance of charters for interstate and international commerce. The House may impose restrictions, sanctions and revocations of charters for trade practices that are contrary to the sovereignty and welfare of citizens or the states.

Section 3.

1. Vacancies in the House of Representatives from any State, shall be filled by an election of the citizens to be held within 4 weeks of the vacancy.

2. The House of Representatives shall choose their own rules of civil procedure and elect their own executive officers every 2 years.

Section 4.

1. The House of Representatives shall have the sole power of initiating an impeachment of any elected representative or senior executive of the National Government whose position was filled by Congressional approval.

2.	Upon a petition of 50% of the elected representatives, the House may convene a committee of impeachment to consider a true bill of indictment. The true bill must state the national felony committed and be ratified by 60% of the total number of representatives.

Section 5. The Authority of the National Senate.

The Senate of the Democratic Republic of America shall be composed of one Senator elected from each state.

The Senators represent the collective corporate interests of the state.

The Senators are chosen every fourth year by the people of the several states.

No elected Senator may serve more than two terms in the same office, nor more than 10 years in the same office, during a lifetime.

No citizen shall be a Senator who shall not have attained to the age of twenty one, and shall have been a citizen of the Democratic Republic of America, for the previous 10 years, and who shall have been a resident of that state for the previous 10 years.

The Senate shall chose their own rules of civil procedure, and elect their other officers every two years.

Vacancies in the Senate from any state, shall be filled by an election of the citizens to be held within 4 weeks of the vacancy.

The Senate shall have the sole power to try all true bills of impeachment, transmitted to the Senate from the House of Representatives.

The true bill of impeachment must state the national crime committed by the accused, including the crime of treason and the crime of espionage against private citizens of the Democratic Republic of America.

A conviction of the accused by two-thirds of the Senate shall result in immediate removal of the officer from office, with a forfeiture of all accrued and future benefits of the office.

Section 6. National Congressional Elections.

The times, places and manner of holding elections for Senators and Representatives, shall be prescribed in each state by the legislature thereof, according to the results of the enumeration of verified citizens in each state, every five years, conducted by the House of Representatives. The state legislature has authority to determine the verification of the qualification of a citizen to vote.

Section 7. Voting.

The members of the House and Senate shall be the judge of the legitimacy of elections, returns and qualifications of its own members.

Upon a petition from any member, or upon a petition from a citizens Grand Jury, the members of the House and Senate shall punish and remove a member for disorderly conduct upon a conviction vote of 60% of the members of the respective House or Senate.

The deliberations of both houses are open public records and procedures, to be broadcast or transmitted to the public on a frequent, periodic basis.

Neither House, during the session of the National Congress, shall, without the consent of the other, adjourn for more than three days. A session of Congress begins on January 21, of each year, adjourns for the month of August, and resumes the first Monday in September, and is in session until December 20, of each year.

Section 8. Compensation.

The Senators and Representatives shall receive compensation for their services, to be ascertained every 10 years, and confirmed by a majority vote of a Grand Jury of 18 citizens, impaneled in the election district of the representative.

No Senator or Representative shall, during the time for which he was elected, be appointed to any civil office of the Democratic Republic of America, nor be entitled to any civil emoluments, and no person holding any civil office in the Democratic Republic of America, shall be an elected member of either House during his term of civil service, nor shall he be a candidate for any office, during his term of civil service.

No Senator or Representative may be appointed to serve as an employee of the National Government for a period of 3 years, after the term of office ends.

Section 9. National Budget and Money.

The National Congress will operate the Democratic Republic of America according to a balanced budget, during a budget cycle of two years, where the expenditures of the Government do not exceed the tax revenues set to meet those expenditures.

The National Government budget, and all bills for raising revenue, shall originate in the Senate, to be completed no later than the day before the August adjournment.

Every budget bill which shall have passed the Senate shall be transmitted to the House. The House must vote on the proposed budget of the Senate by November 30, of each year, or the national budget will revert to the same budget as the previous 2 years.

A budget passed by the House, and the proposed rate of taxes to meet the budget, must be presented to the President of the Democratic Republic of America on December 1, to approve or reject, by December 20 of each year. Upon a rejection by the President, the budget reverts to the same budget as the previous 2 years.

The National Congress shall have power to lay and collect taxes, duties, imposts and excises, to meet the expenditures of the 2 year balanced budget. All duties, imposts and excises shall be uniform throughout the Democratic Republic of America.

No tax or duty shall be laid on articles exported from any state to another state.

No State shall enter into any trade treaty, or trade alliance with a foreign nation.

The National Congress shall have the power to issue government bonds, and to borrow money on the credit of the Democratic Republic of America. All proposals to borrow money or issue debt shall occur once in the two year budget cycle, and all proposals to issue debt must be approved by 50% of the State legislatures of the Democratic Republic of America, no later than January 21 of the year of issuance.

The term of debt and interest on any issuance of debt shall not exceed 10 years, and must be paid in full by the end of the 10th year.

The National Congress shall have the power to regulate commerce and

approve trade agreements with foreign nations, which are negotiated by the President.

The National Congress shall have the power to establish a uniform rule of citizen naturalization, and provide revenues for national border security to prohibit illegal entrance into the sovereign nation or any sovereign state.

The National Congress shall have the power to coin money, regulate the value thereof, regulate the circulation and creation of money and money instruments, regulate the national banking system and establish the currency value of foreign coin, and fix the Standard of Weights and Measures.

The National Congress shall have the power to provide for the punishment for the national criminal felony of counterfeiting the securities and money of the Democratic Republic of America.

The National Congress shall have the power to establish a national Post Office and a national system of roads and transportation routes.

The National Congress shall have the power to authorize regional capital securities markets, and to establish regulatory guidelines for the operation of regional private and public security exchanges designed to promote maximum national and regional economic growth rates.

The National Congress shall have the power to establish and maintain a national patent office to promote the progress of science and useful arts, by securing for limited times to authors and inventors the exclusive right to their respective writings and discoveries.

The National Congress shall have the power to protect the patents of citizens from foreign and domestic criminal usurpation of the right of citizens to enjoy the benefits of their invention.

The National Congress shall have the power to define and punish intellectual property piracies and criminal patent felonies committed against citizens of the Democratic Republic of America by foreign and domestic criminals.

Upon a presentment of a declaration of war by the President, the National Congress shall have the power to declare war and authorize the application of military power and action against foreign enemies, within 2 days of receiving the President's declaration. No military action undertaken by the President may continue after 48 hours, without the consent of the National Congress.

The National Congress shall have the power to raise and support the military and armed forces, to provide and maintain a Navy, and to arm and provide a Coast Guard to protect and preserve the sovereign borders of the Democratic Republic of America.

The National Congress shall have the power to provide for organizing, and arming, the National Guard, and reserving to the states respectively, the appointment of the officers, and the authority of training the National Guard, according to the rules and laws prescribed by the National Congress.

The National Congress shall have the power to make all laws which shall be necessary and proper for carrying into execution the foregoing military powers.

The President shall be the Supreme Commander in Chief of all military personnel and resources.

The National Congress shall have the power to protect the citizen's right of the Writ of Habeas Corpus, which shall not be suspended, unless in case of invasion, when the public safety may require it.

The National Congress is prohibited from passing or enforcing any bill of attainder or ex post facto law.

The National Congress shall have Power to dispose of and make all needful rules and regulations respecting the territory or other property belonging to the Democratic Republic of America; and nothing in this Constitution shall be so construed as to prejudice any claims of the Democratic Republic, or of any particular state.

Article II. The Office of President.

Section 1. Term Limits and Election.

The executive power of the National Government shall be vested in a President of the Democratic Republic of America. He shall hold his office for a term of four years, and, may serve a second term, if elected.

It is the constitutional duty of the President to preserve, protect and defend the natural and civil rights of citizens and to defend the sovereign borders of the nation from foreign and domestic threats.

No President may serve more than two terms, and no more than 10 years during a lifetime.

No Person except a natural born citizen, or a verified Citizen of the Democratic Republic of America for the previous 10 years, shall be eligible for election of President; The President must be at least 35 years of age on the date of assuming office.

The President selects the candidate of Vice President, no later than August 1, of the year of the Presidential election.

The national election for President is held during the two days of the first weekend in November.

The presidential candidate with a majority of electoral college votes is declared the winner, by the House of Representatives, no later than November 15 of the year of the election. The number of electors for each State is equal to the whole number of Senators and Representatives to which the State may be entitled in the Congress.

The Electors shall meet in their respective States, and are legally obligated to vote according to the popular vote of the citizens.

The term of office for the President begins December 1 of the year of the election.

Before he enters office on December 1, the President must recite, in a public ceremony, administered by the House of Representatives, the opening Paragraphs of the Declaration of Independence:

When in the Course of human events it becomes necessary for one people to dissolve the political bands which have connected them with another and to assume among the powers of the earth, the separate and equal station to which the Laws of Nature and of Nature's God entitle them, a decent respect to the opinions of mankind requires that they should declare the causes which impel them to the separation.

I hold these truths to be self-evident, that all men are created equal, that they are endowed by their Creator with certain unalienable Rights, that among these are Life, Liberty and the pursuit of Happiness. — That to secure these rights, Governments are instituted among Men, deriving their just powers from the consent of the governed, — That whenever any Form of Government becomes destructive of these ends, it is the Right of the People to alter or to abolish it, and to institute new Government, laying its foundation on such principles and organizing its powers in such form, as to them shall seem most likely to effect their Safety and Happiness.

Upon the conclusion of reciting the Declaration, The President swears the following oath of office:

I do solemnly swear that I will faithfully execute the Office of President of the Democratic Republic of America, according to the principles of government stated in the Constitution of the Democratic Republic of America.

I solemnly swear to preserve, protect and defend the natural and civil rights of citizens and to defend the sovereign borders of the nation from foreign and domestic threats.

So Help me, God.

Section 2. Removal.

In case of the removal of the President from Office, or of his death, resignation, impeachment, or inability to discharge the powers and duties of the Office, the Vice President assumes the office of President, no later than 24 hours after the removal of the President.

The House of Representatives, by law, may provide for the designation of an interim President, in the event that both the President and Vice President are not able to serve the Office. Within 24 hours of appointing an interim President, the House of Representatives shall set the time and conditions of the election of a new President, by a vote of valid citizens in each state, to be held within 30 days of the appointment of the interim President.

Section 3. General Powers and Authority.

The President shall be the Supreme Commander in Chief of the Army and Navy of the Democratic Republic, and of the National Guard of the several States, when called into the actual service of the Democratic Republic; he may require the opinion, in writing, of the principal officer in each of the military departments, upon any subject relating to the duties of their respective offices.

The President shall have power to grant reprieves and pardons for offences against the Democratic Republic of America, except in cases of impeachment of any national official.

The President shall have power, by and with the advice and consent of the Senate, to make treaties, provided two thirds of the Senators present concur; and he shall nominate, and by and with the advice and consent of the Senate, appoint ambassadors, other public ministers and consuls, and all other Executive Officers of the Democratic Republic of America, whose appointments are not herein otherwise provided for, and which shall be established by law: but the Congress may by law vest the appointment of such inferior officers, as they think proper, in the President alone, in the executive officers of the executive departments.

The President shall have the power to fill all executive vacancies that may happen during the recess of the National Congress, by granting commissions which shall expire at the resumption of the session of the National Congress.

He shall, on January 21 of each year, present to the National Congress, the State of the Union, and recommend to their consideration such measures as he shall judge necessary and expedient for the next two years, including his proposal for the two year budget of the Democratic Republic of America.

The President, Vice President and all civil officers whose appointment to office is confirmed by the National Congress, shall be subject to impeachment for treason against the sovereign interests of the nation or the sovereign interests of the states, espionage against verified citizens, bribery by a foreign government, or other national felony.

Article III. The National Judicial Courts.

Section 1. National Court System.

The national judicial courts shall consist of National District Courts and the National Supreme Court.

The Senate ordains and establishes National District Courts in each state, and provides the two year operating budget for each District Court, every two years.

All judges shall hold a term of office for six years, and may serve one additional term, if approved by the Senate.

No judge may serve more than two terms in a single court system, nor more than 18 years in both courts, in a lifetime.

Vacancies on either the District of Supreme Court are filled by nominations by the Senate, and confirmed by a majority vote of the House of Representatives. The Senate is obligated to nominate judges within 7 days of a vacancy, and the House must confirm or reject the nomination within 7 days of obtaining the nomination from the Senate.

Section 2. National District Courts.

The judicial power of the District and Supreme Court extends to cases arising under the Constitution of the Democratic Republic of America.

The District Court is a trier of facts in criminal and civil cases arising under this Constitution.

In all cases arising in the District Court, the principles of justice are the equal application of the law to all citizens and substantive due process.

The trial of all national crimes shall be by jury, upon a presentment of a true bill of indictment to the District Court, by a majority vote of an impaneled Grand Jury of 18 citizens, in the state where the alleged crime occurred.

A person charged in any state with treason, a national felony, or any other crime against a Congressional law, who shall flee from justice, and be found in another state or foreign nation, shall on demand of the judicial authority of the National District Court, be delivered to the state having jurisdiction of the crime.

The District Court tries cases of treason of citizens against the Democratic Republic of America, or against any Liberty State.

The National Congress shall have the power to declare the punishment of treason, including the penalty of death.

Appeals of judicial decisions from the District to the Supreme Court must state the specific text of the Constitution that is being appealed. A majority of the Supreme Court may agree to hear an appeal.

A decision by the Supreme Court becomes the supreme law of the land for issues pertaining exclusively to the Constitution of the Democratic Republic of America.

This Constitution, and the laws made by the National Congress, or which shall be made, under the Authority of the Democratic Republic, shall be the supreme Law of the Land for laws and cases exclusively pertaining to the National Government.

Full Faith and Credit shall be given in each state to the public acts, records, and judicial proceedings of every other state. And the Senate of the National Congress may by general laws prescribe the manner in which such acts, records and proceedings shall be proved, and the effect thereof.

Section 3. Citizen Grand Jury.

The Chief District Judge manages and administers the Citizen Grand Juries in each district, provides for their operating budget, impanels them and instructs the members that their mission is to serve as a barrier to oppression and tyranny.

Section 4. Qualifications.

All national court judges must be at least 45 years of age, and have been a practicing, licensed attorney at the state or national level, for a period of 20 years, prior to the nomination to the Court.

The mandatory retirement age of all National judges is 70 years of age.

Article IV. Admission of New States and Removal of States From the Union.

Upon a petition for admission from a state legislature, new states may be admitted by the Senate into this Union.

The Senate may determine the geographical area and jurisdiction of a new State, including partial jurisdictions of states not currently a member of this Union.

Verified citizens of a partial jurisdiction in any state not in the Union may petition the Senate based upon a certified referendum of 66% of the citizens in the proposed jurisdiction.

Prior to their admission to the Union, as a condition of admission, the state or partial jurisdiction, seeking admission must deposit a full year of their projected taxes into the National Treasury, as determined by the Senate.

Upon a resolution presented by a Senator of any state, the national Congress may consider the removal of an existing state member of the Union.

The grounds for removal are failure to abide by the rules of this Constitution.

A vote of 2/3 of the representatives of all states is sufficient for permanent removal from the Union, effective immediately upon the vote.

Any state may secede from this Union by a petition ratified by a majority of the state legislature, presented to the National Senate.

The Senate must act upon the petition to grant secession within 14 days.

The grant of secession is irrevocable and permanent.

Notwithstanding the permanency of secession of a state, verified citizens of a partial geographical territory of the former state may petition the Senate for admission as a new state.

A citizen of the Democratic Republic of America may emigrate to a non-member territory or state by a petition of citizenship revocation.

A citizen revocation of citizenship is irrevocable and permanent.

Article V. Amendments.

Upon a petition from any state legislature to the Senate, a resolution for amendment of this Constitution may be considered by both houses of the National Congress.

The resolution must be voted upon within 14 days of submission to the National Congress.

A vote of 2/3 of the representatives of both houses, from all states, enacts the amendment, which becomes effective immediately.

A failed resolution of the amendment may not be reconsidered by the National Congress for a period of 5 years after the date of the vote.

About Laurie Thomas Vass.

Laurie Thomas Vass is a North Carolina constitutional economist.

Vass is a graduate of the University of North Carolina at Chapel Hill and has an undergraduate degree in Political Science and a Masters degree in Regional Planning.

She was a professional money manager with her own investment advisory firm for 30 years, and was cited by Peter Tanous, in The Wealth Equation, as one of the top 100 private managers in the nation.

She is the inventor and holder of a research method patent on selecting technology stocks for investment accounts.

Vass is the author of ten books, and over 100 scholarly economic articles on the Social Science Research Network author platform. She is currently ranked in the top 1.3% of over 420,000 economic authors, worldwide, on the SSRN platform.

Her articles on the SSRN platform are available for free.

She is a student of North Carolina history and public policy, and her books and articles about the state are archived in the Carolina Collection, at Wilson Library, at UNC.

All of her books are available for purchase at GabbyPress.com

www.ingramcontent.com/pod-product-compliance
Lightning Source LLC
Chambersburg PA
CBHW070913030426
42336CB00014BA/2391